RESET

Rethinking Our World
and Creating
a Different Future

PHILIPP KRISTIAN DIEKHÖNER

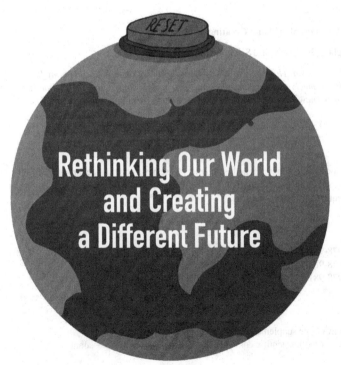

Rethinking Our World
and Creating
a Different Future

 **World Scientific**

NEW JERSEY · LONDON · SINGAPORE · BEIJING · SHANGHAI · HONG KONG · TAIPEI · CHENNAI · TOKYO

Published by

World Scientific Publishing Co. Pte. Ltd.

5 Toh Tuck Link, Singapore 596224

USA office: 27 Warren Street, Suite 401-402, Hackensack, NJ 07601

UK office: 57 Shelton Street, Covent Garden, London WC2H 9HE

Library of Congress Control Number: 2021015322

British Library Cataloguing-in-Publication Data
A catalogue record for this book is available from the British Library.

RESET
Rethinking Our World and Creating a Different Future

ISBN 978-981-122-754-7 (hardcover)
ISBN 978-981-122-755-4 (ebook for institutions)
ISBN 978-981-122-756-1 (ebook for individuals)

For any available supplementary material, please visit
https://www.worldscientific.com/worldscibooks/10.1142/12023#t=suppl

Typeset by Diacritech Technologies Pvt. Ltd.
Chennai - 600106, India

Printed in Singapore

For our future children and the wonderful world we could give them.

CONTENTS

hello
world

FOREWORD
The year nobody expected

I t's fair to say COVID-19 turned the world upside down quite a bit. The hardships many of us suffered during this unprecedented time are worthy of the utmost recognition and empathy. But as the eternal optimist that I am, despite feeling the impact, what I've gained is perspective (and probably weight). Yes, I *do* choose to see a silver lining in the food for thought it gives us, and I'm the first to say yes to a degustation of something new and strange. However tragic the global unfolding of this pandemic, it offers unique insight into the downsides of our hyper-globalised world and the often-calcified systems upholding it. These issues are more urgent and

> However tragic the global unfolding of this pandemic, it offers unique insight into the downsides of our hyper-globalised world and the often-calcified systems upholding it.

obvious than ever, which gives us a pristine opportunity to address them – for *our* future.

As I write these words on a sprawling sunny day in Italy baking in the dry heat, having invested my savings in a sabbatical of *sprezzatura*, I find myself reflecting on how COVID-19 changed our lives. How might it lead to something good? For many of us, it's nudged us to rethink, return to our roots, challenge our outlook on life, and hopefully emerge wiser from it.

When I started writing *The Trust Economy*, I knew something interesting was happening with our world and with us. It took me plenty of time to express my hunch on what exactly that was, a perspective spawn from many years of fascination with trust and how its presence can drive humanity forward. But this book is different. This is a look ahead at what might be in store for us and how we take ownership of that future. It's an optimistic rallying call for all of us to respond to the neon writing on the wall that is COVID-19. Mother Earth may have acutely fallen ill with COVID, but she's already been chronically disposed to ill-health, plagued by the problems that we as humans have created – by example, climate change and geopolitical mayhem.

The root causes? Bad habits and a fixation on treating symptoms while ignoring their causes. As we're gradually waking to the downsides of this global condition, profound transformation is making its way to shore. While we ride this global storm, we can only hope it will clear the air for a better world ahead. What's certain is that a new orientation for our global humanity is increasingly inevitable. We like to overestimate the pace of mega-change arising but underestimate its magnitude. Doing so reflects our human nature to stick to old habits, even when something promising is on the horizon. But humankind frequently surprises itself. My hunch is that much of the change awaiting us is actually a return to things that are inherently human.

As we take a look at what got us to where we are today and subsequently where we will go from here, we must understand human nature is a potent foundation from which all sorts of things can manifest. Unfortunately, the more we put systems in place that detach us from the people we share our lives with and lead us to distrust our fellow folks, the less likely it is that we will lean toward the good. Once we take a closer look at how we interact and transact with each other globally, we discover a consequential amount of friction. To this effect, it shouldn't be a surprise when many of our attempts at solving problems on a global scale yield little more than hot air. That friction gets in the way of our well-being and necessary change. It isn't *us*, and it also isn't *them*. It's the systems we encapsulated ourselves in that are now blocking our path ahead. Most of those systems were initially built with good intentions – and *for* collaboration – but have failed us on multiple fronts, outgrowing the original needs which were their *raison d'être*. Many have unfortunately triggered antagonism within us, both against said systems and our fellow people.

Just think about the last time you received a pointless fine or fought customer service team. It leaves people on the in- and

> We ought to stop telling ourselves that life is about trading off because that depreciates the ingenuity which got us here in the first place.

outsides frustrated, exhausted, and disillusioned. Humanity operates at an order of magnitude where we can no longer afford to play win-lose games and pretend that it doesn't take all of us to build our future. We ought to stop telling ourselves that life is about trading off because that depreciates the ingenuity which got us here in the first place. It's time this stops once and for all, and to start something new.

Humans have always known to use their social intelligence to make sure one and one equalled three. When we speak about change these days, sentiments tend to focus on what we lose instead of what we stand to gain. Only those looking past legacy see light on the horizon. This, in itself, could be a problem as it elucidates how we've gridlocked ourselves into a situation too large to manage for the tools we have in our arsenal today. It might mean we are confined to seeing change as a trade-off and this discernment needs to change. COVID-19 has turned the world upside down. But what lies beyond the ruins of the unprecedented disaster we've all just faced is an opportunity to ask the questions we really need answered. Those questions should make us wonder why a pandemic like this can bring large parts of our human civilisation to a halt. What did, and didn't we do, that led us here?

> COVID-19 has turned the world upside down. But what lies beyond the ruins of the unprecedented disaster we've all just faced is an opportunity to ask the questions we really need answered.

This book is a collection of pivotal ideas and behaviours I dissected, applied, and taught throughout my innovation and transformation work with Fortune 500s, technology disruptors and public institutions. Much of it reflects the many enlightening conversations I've had with people from all walks of life, with thinkers and dreamers like yourselves. Its purpose is to help us fix the broken and create a brighter future together – particularly in the context of a post-COVID world awaiting us on the horizon. Come with me on a journey to answers for the big riddles of our times. Let's hope that we rediscover our humanity and work towards a new social and economic order turning gratitude for humanity and our planet into our core modus operandi.

As I find myself distracted by a butterfly gently landing on a lavender bush in full summer bloom, I wish more than ever that this new normal will serve as a reminder for us to appreciate our very own nature and the beauty that surrounds us. I look forward to enacting this exponentially greater future with you, my clientele, and the many wonderful people I encounter on my path on this beautiful planet. May this book surprise and delight you with its melody of pragmatic storytelling, dry humour, and pinch of idealistic unreasonableness on which every great transformation rests. I trust you will connect the dots, and you're welcome to share your ideas and perspectives with me via *pk@philippkristian.com.*

May this book surprise and delight you with its melody of pragmatic storytelling, dry humour, and pinch of idealistic unreasonableness on which every great transformation rests.

In keeping with a tradition started in the Foreword of *The Trust Economy*, I want to highlight here that I lay no claim to present absolute – let alone full – truth in this book. Our world and its knowledge are way too vast for me to do that. That being said, even our fragmented understanding of the whole can mobilise great change and transform our world for the better. I really hope and wish the future of humanity will sound like a mixtape of its greatest hits rather than a cheap cover album of antiquated anthems. It's time to reset towards a new and improved *us*. Together, we'll emerge stronger from it all.

Yours faithfully,
Philipp Kristian Diekhöner

I

the big reset

'Being in a land of opportunity is of little merit if you are in a state of denial.'

Chapter 1

THE CATALYST
How we got here and why it matters

W e're social creatures. It doesn't take a global pandemic to appreciate this, but it does take some digging to appreciate just how integral our gregarious tendencies are to our identity as humankind. We're hyper-social because that is our greatest competitive edge over all other biomass on Earth. All our sentience and brain power are best deployed doing what we are arguably better at than anything else on this planet: cooperate for collective gain. According to a study in *Nature Communications*, a leading scientific journal:

> *"Proactive, that is, unsolicited, prosociality is a key component of our hyper-cooperation, which in turn has enabled the emergence of various uniquely human traits, including complex cognition, morality and cumulative culture and technology."*[1]

One of the world's most widely-cited academic contributions to the field of sociology, a paper by Mark S. Granovetter titled "The Strength of Weak Ties",[2] argues that we're particularly good at building bridges between separate closely-knit social groups, thereby creating a vast network in which we can benefit from one another. This is accomplished without the need to divert too much attention away from our core *'tribe'.*

The idea is that by bridging between different social circles through 'weak ties' (e.g., acquaintances), we advance social capital both ways and weave large-scale networks of collaboration. When we begin casting our net into other social circles, it doesn't take long to realise just how mutual the benefits are.

Social capital is an informal human system accounting for our efforts in helping others. To this effect, we fear adverse effects to our well-being by focusing on that of others could be considered irrational because looking out for one another can actually serve us better than self-absorption. Reciprocating and repaying favours seem natural to us and makes us stronger together. Your biology teacher may have referred to this concept as 'symbiosis' and perhaps explained it with an example of a fungus and tree exchanging nutrients for mutual gain and survival. But if the fungus and tree don't end up becoming friends in a mutually beneficial way, we must take it as a transactional arrangement. Humanity has demonstrated that it is capable of far more than that by shifting the nature of the transaction from default arrangements by necessity to intentional *relationships by choice.* We're so wired to be social that we tend to treat others

> We're so wired to be social that we tend to treat others fairly even when there's no reputational repercussions for doing otherwise.

fairly even when there's no reputational repercussions for doing otherwise (take that, selfish gene theory!). Our genes may be selfish all they want, but our lives aren't – or they shouldn't be. As another article on the matter puts it:

> *"Cooperation increases group productivity and/or survival and hence provides a direct benefit to individuals who cooperate."*[3]

Sophisticated social teamwork is the underlying narrative of our human success story. Cooperation has played a far greater role in humanity dominating the Earth than did blunt aggression. We owe our ultra-cooperative nature to psychological mechanisms enabling us to live peacefully in large social groups. Many animal species also do this. Primates (e.g., chimpanzees) and insects like ants and honeybees are known for their social nature, which affords them many advantages. Competition often gets in the way of that. As an article concludes, controlling competition is *"fundamental to the evolution and maintenance of cooperative relationships".*[4] It elaborates that:

> *"Our species is routinely depicted as unique in its ability to achieve cooperation, whereas our closest relative, the chimpanzee (Pan troglodytes), is often characterized as overly competitive."*[5]

If we reflect on this for a moment in the context of the often hyper-competitive socio-economic realities we exist in, are we really still worthy of such praise? In the case of chimpanzees, behaviours including mutual grooming, group hunting and food sharing co-exist with competition for resources and sexual partners – not much unlike what we humans are accustomed to. Individuals and coalitions are subject to dominance hierarchies that maintain social order. But primarily, such teamwork is transactional. The bounty of a chimpanzee troop's hunt isn't divided equally; it's a full-blown competition for food. To us humans, this approach may seem unfair and short-sighted. But so increasingly is our global economy. Where does that leave us?

In many ways, we evolved far beyond such primitive approaches to collaboration, establishing a sense of belonging to our social groups and complex interdependencies on those foundations. Collaboration of this sort is usually a positive-sum game. Except, of course, the courtesy does not always extend to those outside of *'our'* group. Ironically, collaboration serves also to defend our group territory against 'others'. The hormone oxytocin appears to play a major role in this. Colloquially known as the 'love hormone', oxytocin has been argued to influence how we cooperate.[6,7] It tends to increase harmony *within* groups and hostility towards other groups at the same time. Such social dynamics promote putting group above individual, but at the expense of non-group individuals. What at first looks like a prosocial win-win situation turns into a rather hostile scenario once we zoom the picture out.

With this, the more cohesive a group identity, the more exclusively it operates on the inside and the more adversely it responds to outsiders. In other words, the more you trust your tribe, the less you trust 'other' tribes. Cooperation is hard and full of friction when based on a precedent of distrust, leading people to favour their immediate cohort for collaboration. But when distrust both defines and creates a barrier between others and us, our world view becomes narrowed and skewed. This parochial perception deters us from realising the bigger picture. The definitive divide perpetuated by distrust creates a self-imposed trap, held together by legacy systems and archaic thinking in dire need of a major update.

Contradicting this dynamic, however, are individuals with an innate ability to cooperate universally and whose cooperation *"transcends group boundaries"*.[8] In large part, this falls on the role that reputation plays when added to the mix. We are more inclined to collaborate with out-group individuals when it benefits our reputation. Social capital(-ism) paints a picture in which we can trade and 'bank' favours with diverse groups of people, harmonising our pursuit of individual and shared benefits through this indirect form of reciprocity. The strength of weak ties, then, is the story of how overcoming that barrier brings great benefits to humanity. This is where the magic happens. Large-scale sophisticated cooperation is what makes us such a successful life form.

Indeed, humanity has managed to overcome many of its inter-tribal hostilities over time. At some point, we put down the axe and focused on trading. We eventually built an interconnected society by conducting business – more or less productively – with one another. On an economic level, we have managed to, largely and universally, trust in the same basic concepts. First and foremost, that is capital. And yet, to this day, we still struggle with trusting the people behind those exchanges of capital.

> On an economic level, we have managed to, largely and universally, trust in the same basic concepts. First and foremost, that is capital. And yet, to this day, we still struggle with trusting the people behind those exchanges of capital.

Our world might still feel like a patchwork of more or less sizeable hostile tribes but at least we are now connected by reasonably robust global transactional networks. While they do work reasonably well, they're pathologically skewed in terms of power and value distribution. Money gives us enough of a shared baseline to trade globally, but this doesn't necessarily extend into bringing us closer socially or caring for each other in an equitable and reciprocal fashion. In essence, once we have made our money from the stranger or foreigner, we immediately *stop* caring – at least our capitalist selves are trained to. Such lack of trust and care in *people* we place instead a shared interest in *money*. Placing trust in the collective desire for money *over* the people revolving around it fuels inequity and creates a divide. It's perhaps convenient, but an issue if we want to ensure humanity can build a shared stewardship of Earth on more than transactions. We owe this to our intelligence, ingenuity, and future generations.

Human collaboration at-scale has become almost synonymous with capital, a highly pervasive creation of human imagination which essentially assigns value to things. Capital is a form of scalable memory and storage for value, so to speak. This value is abstract, meaning that its inherent value reveals itself *in the context in which it is used*. For example, if you own $100, you own the power of converting that money into, say, a basket of groceries, a date night, a budget airline flight, a personal yoga session, or whatever else you would like to purchase. This means the greenback offers a promise of value *once you convert it* into something. You happily hold onto it because you know you can turn it into something of your choosing anytime you like. However, in itself, the green piece of paper has little *intrinsic use* of its own. The reason this is possible is because we have formed a universal shared idea of the value stored in a $100 note (or its digital equivalent in your bank account).

This universal trust in the value of money has made it easy to collaborate, because it created common ground and understanding on which to do so. Prior to the invention of money, the whole ordeal was a more abstract process to acquire what we needed or wanted from others. Under a bartering system, if you had an ox and needed a handful of eggs, the trade would be exceedingly convoluted and based entirely on subjectivity. But with this subjectivity comes the intent and importance of fairness. Fairness has always mattered, simply because reciprocity is a good strategy when you co-exist with others. We are wired for it. But getting this right was more difficult before money came to the scene.

Imagine the inconvenience of having to barter back and forth while keeping a record of who owed what to whom, while taking into account certain hierarchies which might skew favours towards one or the other. All of this broadly falls into the gambit of social capital. Money made this dynamic much simpler, establishing a common denominator to express the possession of value and enable it to be traded easily. Money made exchanges of value universally *tradable*. It's merely a more explicit, and less personal, form of the accounting that we innately perform in our social circles to this day. Even now, we might utilise money to purchase eggs, but the egg supplier might gladly forfeit payment if you were to introduce a business connection, with an understanding that we earned social capital if we did our job well. But irrespective of whether money is involved or not, the way we account for socio-economic collaboration makes us a remarkable species.

The ability of capital to facilitate human cooperation becomes ubiquitously supercharged when we introduce a time axis to the conversation. For instance, our friend with the ox might suggest a deal to his chosen egg supplier. For a daily supply of five eggs over the course of a year, he would agree to trade in his ox upfront. We commonly refer to this as *credit*. Credit, broadly, is the trust someone extends to another in providing something whose value will be repaid in time to come. While this is similar to social capital in the sense that favours may not be immediately reciprocated, credit is relatively transactional bound by explicit terms. However, with this, there is inherent downside risk, prompting the credit provider to desire security in the form of collateral and further negotiate favourable terms in exchange for their extension of credit. This commonly takes the form of *interest*. Our proud ox owner may negotiate to receive more eggs for his ox in total than he would if the transaction were settled all at once. Since the egg supplier may not, at any given point in time, stock enough eggs to buy an ox, and the ox owner probably doesn't have use for thousands of eggs all at once, the two form a win-win situation. So much for the theory, the equivalent of which we see in practice through countless daily transactions of this sort.

But things *could* go wrong. The ox could turn out to be weaker than promised, or it could die on its first day on the new job. The egg supplier might fail to deliver the eggs, offer bad quality or close shop due to unforeseen circumstances after some time. All of this uncertainty comprises the transactional risk involved. In order for things to go smoothly, this risk needs to be mitigated. A neutral middleman could enter the picture to vet both sides, spell out the terms of the credit agreement for each, and oversee the entire transaction until it is completed. In exchange, the middleman would be compensated for offering his services of intermediation (intermediation logically stems from inter, meaning 'in between', and mediation, i.e., facilitation). He might even be the one to introduce the two parties in the first place, initiating the transaction to take place.

Our egg supplier could receive his ox and rent him onwards as a working animal to a chicken farmer in need of transporting his produce. In exchange for this, the chicken farmer might agree to provide the egg supplier with seven extra eggs daily in payment. One of those eggs becomes payment for the middleman, and the others becomes an additional asset for the egg supplier, which he can use at his discretion. Trust and credit intermediation for a fee of the kind here described in simple terms is what financial systems are fundamentally built on. With money assuming the place of bartering, this entire activity becomes much more objective because of the currency system that we have established for money to universally be traded beyond borders. This illustrates the magical interaction of capital and human collaboration. It's one of the reasons we visit chimpanzees in zoos nowadays, instead of the other way around.

> This illustrates the magical interaction of capital and human collaboration. It's one of the reasons we visit chimpanzees in zoos nowadays, instead of the other way around.

The human-made magic of capital and collaboration have been foundational to our progress in recent centuries, but so is the role of technology, as well as the imagination and ingenuity with which we build in ideas, concepts, solutions, and systems existing independent of the physical world and on a basis of shared universal trust in them. In a world where animals are confined to experiencing the physical world and their own being, humanity can interact with brands, corporations, governments, nations and much more of which only makes sense in our collective imagination. Interaction on this level fuels an extraordinary ability to organise in great numbers, realise monumental undertakings and innovate with a spirit of discovery.

Building and maintaining settlements of millions of people coexisting is an extraordinary achievement and miracle of this unique human spiderweb of meaning. It has allowed us to progress unlike any other species on Earth. We can trace this dam of formalisation (and later, globalisation) to the shift from foraging to agriculture many thousands of years ago. Life changed profoundly, and, aside all gains, came with its drawbacks. Hunter-gatherers were generalists, and agriculture began to transition people towards specialisation. It brought with it a more structured approach to cooperation, and enabled population growth. But with increasing population density, infectious disease spread more easily, seasonal hunger and malnutrition emerged due to greater reliance on far fewer crops with specific harvest seasons – and further perpetuated social hierarchies and inequalities. As one assessment on the subject summarises:

"This trend towards declining health was observed for 19 of 21 societies undergoing the agricultural transformation. The counterintuitive increase in nutritional diseases resulted from seasonal hunger, reliance on single crops deficient in essential nutrients, crop blights, social inequalities, and trade."[9]

Farming, in fact, wasn't a straightforward choice from a human welfare standpoint. Another study on the matter found hunter-gatherer societies to suffer less from famines than agricultural ones. Their ability to migrate to greener pastures in case of drought or other negative influences gave them an edge we would likely refer to today as 'agility'.[10]

Aside from food shortages, surpluses also became a problem. Natural human preference for calorically dense foods containing high fat and sugar was useful in foraging times when their availability was unpredictable at best. It became a liability when access increased due to preferential farming of such crops.[11]

Many of these health effects became permanent, even altering our genome. As one Harvard Medical School study found, *"genetic selection occurred along with the changes in lifestyle and demography, and that selection continued to happen following the transition"*.[12] Some of the changes were apparently very visible, indeed: *"The impact of agriculture, accompanied by increasing population density and a rise in infectious disease, was observed to decrease stature in populations from across the entire globe and regardless of the temporal period during which agriculture was adopted, including Europe, Africa, the Middle East, Asia, South America, and North America."*

Without reading too deeply into these findings, we do see that innovation tends to create its own offspring in eliciting new problems to emerge – particularly when it involves breakthrough shifts in the way we live, work, and play. Progress has its side effects: the more potent

> We do see that innovation tends to create its own offspring in eliciting new problems to emerge – particularly when it involves breakthrough shifts in the way we live, work, and play.

the good in change, the more pervasive the side-effects. Inevitably, that may have catalysed a snowball effect of even greater and more impactful change as a means of continuously addressing new issues emergent from our previous breakthroughs. This might explain why human progress is so relentless.

As the magnitude of all this progress grows, so does the scope of its adverse consequences. This might explain why our tendency and need for change continues to accelerate. But perhaps that narrative of our advancement isn't a straightforward path – and more likely resemblant of a perpetual back-and-forth between innovation and adaptation. Transformation isn't a direct line from point A to B, even if it may initially seem that way. This is, in large part, because the destination often remains unknown to a certain degree. There's an evident disconnect between what we think the future brings and how it eventually unfolds. It would be foolish to believe we really knew at any given point what was awaiting us. Change happens, and the way it does usually runs counter-intuitive to planning and deliberate adaptation. In reality, we might trick ourselves into believing that our understanding of past transformation enabled us to meticulously plan for the change ahead of us. But this is hardly the case.

Returning to my earlier scenario, agriculture is now a suitable metaphor for the evident disconnect between the promise of a better future and the reality that ensues. As recent as 2019, the University of Cambridge published the results of a study involving the Agta, modern-day hunter-gatherer people in the Philippines. They compared the daily activities of Agta communities focusing on hunting and gathering with those engaging in both foraging and rice farming.

"On average, the team estimate that Agta engaged primarily in farming work around 30 hours per week while foragers only do so for 20 hours (...) The study found that women living in the communities most involved in farming had half as much leisure time as those in communities which only foraged."[13]

While this is just a singular proof point on the subject, it may give rise to the hypothesis that the human transition to agricultural civilisations long ago didn't just create new social problems, but came along with hidden productivity costs, too. As reinforced, what we definitively do know is that agricultural way of life facilitated impressive population growth, which means individual productivity losses were likely overshadowed by a persistent illusion of material prosperity. Growth directs our attention away from relative sacrifices and fixates our attention on absolute gains. This is a problem because productivity actually determines whether our future generations will be economically better off than us. This isn't primarily a question of technological progress as invention only makes things better, in theory. It's primarily a question of the quality and extent of human collaboration.

Endnotes

1   https://www.nature.com/articles/ncomms5747

2   https://www.jstor.org/stable/2776392

3   https://onlinelibrary.wiley.com/doi/full/10.1111/j.1420-9101.2006.01258.x

4   https://www.pnas.org/content/113/36/10215

5   Ibid.

6   https://www.ncbi.nlm.nih.gov/pmc/articles/PMC6347450/

7   https://journals.plos.org/plosone/article?id=10.1371/journal.pone.0046751

8   https://www.pnas.org/content/pnas/114/48/12702.full.pdf

9   https://www.ncbi.nlm.nih.gov/pubmed/21507735

10 https://www.ncbi.nlm.nih.gov/pmc/articles/PMC3917328/

11 Ibid.

12 https://www.sciencedaily.com/releases/2015/11/151123202631.htm

13 https://www.sciencedaily.com/releases/2019/05/190520115646.htm

Chapter 2

ONE FOR THE TEAM
When competition lost to collaboration

Few things drive us as much as the need to belong. Belongingness is increasingly a challenge for people in modern urban environs – a complete contradiction to the hyperconnected world at our disposal. A plausible reason for this is our overreliance on an economic system celebrating competition as a cornerstone of economic health and value creation. Neighbourly relations, communities, and any of the social circles that fulfil our desire to belong also thrive on the absence of direct competition. Few modern cities operate on mutual human support. Residents compete for apartments, jobs, partners, and their chance to be lonely at the top. It would appear that loneliness and mental illness are particularly prevalent amongst big city dwellers – which is incongruent to their surroundings, living amidst masses of people, resources, and infrastructure. Perhaps city-dwellers accept the endless competition across all aspects of life as a trade-off for the amenities of the urban jungles.

What we do know is that hyper-competitive environments remove us from our natural inclination to cooperate. I believe the latent human and economic consequences of this could be thoroughly devastating. Research on the effect that cities have on our mental and overall well-being are conflicted because of the apparent paradox it presents: better infrastructure and healthcare on the one hand, higher incidence and risk for mental conditions on the other.[1] Essentially, most great human achievements are founded on collaboration systems with competition given a role as side-kick at best. As useful as a competition may seem to be for winning say a game of golf, or determining a new group leader, even pro sports is built as much on collaboration as on hard-nosed competition. The lucky golf pro was likely coached, probably enjoys clubs and balls from their brand sponsor of choice and wouldn't even have the chance to partake in a competition without an organising association. All of these are collaborative efforts built around like-minded groups of people with shared trust in achieving a certain objective. Competition may be a visible outcome of all this, but in the grand scheme of things, it plays second violin at best.

This is true even for global trade, which relies on the win–win assumption of mutual gain that incentivises trading to begin with. It also becomes particularly apparent in a game of sports or social situation involving more than one player. Individual competition must be wrapped in a context of collaborative effort for us to avoid it getting in the way of progress forcing us to resort to primitive uncompromising situations in which we face one enemy after another would plain stress us out. By all means, for all the surface-level status and wealth it may afford us (if we're good at it), individual competition hollows us. Moreover, it disproportionately favours problematic and selfish personality traits. In an environment where bad behaviour gets promoted, we're setting ourselves up for collective misery and disaster. I reckon global politics and a fair share of corporate scandals serve as a rich metaphor for this dynamic in action.

Accordingly, our problem isn't competition overall, but rather *individual* competition. Intergroup competition still allows for collaboration *within* the group, whereas individual competition is an 'all against all' scenario. Group-to-group competition may be inevitable or even exciting at times, but only if it remains friendly. When we have the support of our in-group, we can at least choose to spend our energy on supporting over aggressing. To this accord, bridges of support can extend easily from our in-group to an out-group. For instance, one research contribution on the subject found that people were *"reluctant to harm the outgroup after being exposed to the opportunity to help it".*[2] It seems as though people *prefer* to collaborate whenever it is possible – at least as long as it is safe for them and their group to do so. A resounding analysis on the matter found that competitive pressures drive unethical conduct and are more influential in their spread than greed.[3] In other words, the real issue isn't bad-natured people, but the need to react to pressure exerted by the competition. High social capital environments perform better economically *and* socially.[4] Urban environments founded on high social capital, for instance, tend to be safer, cleaner, wealthier, and more liveable.[5] Social capital increases cooperation.

> The real issue isn't bad-natured people, but the need to react to pressure exerted by the competition.

As such, it is now widely recognised that forming strategic alliances can help organisations innovate.[6] With this, it would appear that competition lost to collaboration. Unfortunately, competition is the quintessential bad loser. And to this effect, it continues to exert a rather dysfunctional influence at all levels of society.

But why are our schools, workplaces, social existences, and identities so intrinsically defined by hyper-competition when much of it is counterproductive to our well-being and progress? Competition doesn't encourage peak performance alone, but promotes selfishness, distrust towards other individuals or groups, and a persistent 'winner versus loser' mindset. None of these serve as a good foundation for advancing the future of our species. They sow conflict, ignorance, and hostility. In such an environment, we lose what's most dear to us: belongingness, unity, and a sense of purpose.

Considering that we share a single planet, our focus should hypothetically rest on creating value for all of humanity and distributing it as equitably as possible among those alive. Socio-economic collaboration that ensures fair gains for all involved will overcome the situation where people continue to identify the most challenging global problems as someone else's. We truly need this unity to find answers to – and then effectively resolve – the big problems of our times.

The age-old economic theory of comparative advantage already teaches us that even if we

22

are not *absolutely* the best at everything, we are *relatively* better at some things compared with others – and thus the notion of benefiting from trade with each other is born. Trading is the transactional baseline for human collaboration, making us *relatively* better off. So, will everything just work itself out naturally so long as this is the case?

As with anything, the Achilles heel of any economic theory is its underlying assumptions – and, often, variables that can't be controlled. One of the most disproven, yet pervasive theories presumes that our economic behaviour is rational. In such a scenario, competition could *rationally* make sense and *rationally* lead to the best outcomes by creating incentive and pressure for excellence and advancement. But making the assumption that our economic behaviour is rational is completely *irrational* because, as we very well know, humanity doesn't work that way. For instance, our frame of reference dramatically skews our perceptions, interpretations, and response to any given situation.[7]

Behavioural economics challenge the assumption of individual rationality and much of it is owed to the influence of perception and context.[8] Imagine it like the difference between ordering an iced latte at your favourite brunch spot versus picking one up from the supermarket. You'll experience very different comfort levels for the price of the two largely identical items because of a difference in context, which changes your expectations towards it and, thereby, what you are prepared to pay for it. Also compare a petrol station on the motorway with one right outside the motorway exit. Same petrol, similar logistical effort, but slightly different context and value proposition which leads to an often substantial difference in price. Explaining this variation with a rational take on supply and demand would lead to nowhere.

Context explains what is actually going on and also demonstrates the relativity of our needs, wants, and how they are met in a given context. More precisely, there could be no difference in value proposition without a difference in context. For two identical contexts (which purely exist in theory), two identical items would naturally fetch an identical price. The closest we come to this in reality is when we, say, shop in different branches of the same supermarket chain or dine at different restaurants in a franchise. In order for the value proposition to change, so must the context. This is what great brands excel at and the reason why you pay multiples for branded goods compared to otherwise similar generic alternatives. You're paying more for the ability to trust that your expectation of the brand's promise will be met with each purchase. You're essentially de-risking your choices that way, and that's usually great business. Most context relies on perception which means even a small change in reality can lead to a major change in context. Such contextual leverage is the bedrock of all great value creation and every extraordinary business. When it works, we call this *originality*, and that's something we pay for, however intangible and irrational it may appear under close scrutiny.

But what does this have to do with competition, cooperation, and co-opetition (cooperation between competing players)? A great deal, actually, because it clearly reveals two things: competition relies on a single yardstick for comparison to be effective to any degree. In a 100m sprint, that yardstick is the time every runner achieves on the same standardised ground and distance. In such a scenario, competition can indeed nurture peak performance. But in business, no such normative form of competition exists. Even when two organisations directly compete for the same tender, their contexts are fundamentally different, as will be their propositions.

Competition solely works in fully commoditised goods markets, such as those for raw materials, where a common yardstick does exist. There, it incentivises economic players to compete directly, which can lead to efficiency. But this can also incentivise cutting corners and unethical conduct. For anything more complex and difficult to compare than say a raw material like crude oil, competition gets in the way of business by promoting needless hostility. And, as we know it, this actually hurts productivity.[9] The more intellectual the work, the more competitive incentives hinder actual work performance. This also explains why companies pitted against each other may find their competitiveness is self-sabotaging them into cutting their own flesh. That's because competition makes us more narrow-minded. This is why it tends to exclusively work in driving performance when a simple task is at hand for us to complete with single-minded focus and in the exact same way as everyone we're competing with. As it might be obvious to you by now, no real-world business problem worth solving works like that. Karl Duncker's 1945 candle problem illustrates how competition *increases* functional fixation and *decreases* creative alternative forms of problem solving.

In the aforementioned 100m sprint where a simple task is taken on by a single person, competition may be an appropriate mindset. Competition in sports takes the form of a friendly *'ritualised aggression'* in which the focus is more on the purpose of achieving a meaningful goal than it is on defeating others. We all know what happens when this benign competition loses sight of the target and becomes preoccupied with actual aggression towards the

> Competition becomes particularly dysfunctional when we are competing against *others*, instead of *for* something worthwhile.

opponent. Soccer stadiums full of violent fans may come to mind. Competition becomes particularly dysfunctional when we are competing against *others*, instead of *for* something worthwhile.

Quintessentially, the selfish gene did not create the selfish individual. Sociality is an asset that creates collaboration and in turn makes everyone involved better off. This means prosociality is actually a better strategy than selfishness in making the best of our individual circumstances. Much of this thinking has sadly become lost in modern economic and management systems. A command-and-control culture of 20th century modern management and administrative thinking – baggage we inherited from industrialisation that still defines corporations today – may have derailed our spirit of collaboration in favour of a cult of selfishness. Under this pretence, it may appear that selfishness serves us, but the facts suggest instead that it makes us worse off. That's why nationalism isn't a great idea, even in an age of too much globalisation.

A nation's selfishness is just as problematic as an individual's; a corporation's selfish pursuit of money counterintuitively makes it less successful than it could be. In all of these instances, we're missing the big picture – that what lies beyond our immediate periphery is where we can manifest a greater impact for the whole. But even in daily work routines, command and control has demonstratively thwarted growth in productivity despite exponential advancements in technology. Even here, collaboration ultimately makes more sense. Take that, selfish gene theory!

Yves Morieux[10] and others have observed a decade-by-decade decline in annual productivity gains from several percentage points in the 1970s to less than 1% productivity growth per annum. This suggests we are reaching a ceiling in our current system of productivity. The exponential progress that technology has facilitated in recent decades should have correlatively accelerated productivity in a much more profound way that it has.

Contrary to that, decision-making in many organisations has actually slowed down. More people are being involved in decisions than used to be the case – which can attribute to both infrastructural bureaucracy and accessibility. When an organisation powered by distrust dabbles into new technological possibilities, those will nearly always be utilised for policing people rather than making their lives easier. Under this assumption, business productivity growth is stalling because of the way business culture is utilising technology – not because of its inherent possibilities.[11]

As a result, what we are at risk of witnessing a productivity stagnation in the 2020s to the extent that human obsession with competition and control over collaboration might eventually fully offset technological progress. Like COVID-19, that scenario would be a late, but much needed wake up call. It's become idiomatic for people to complain about how hard it is to 'get stuff done'.[12] Morieux explains this dilemma with an example of a relay race where a team of individually faster runners is outperformed by a team of runners whose individual running performance is far lesser, but who possess superior teamwork. In a world as complex as we face today, interfaces between people (such as the baton handover in a relay race) are mission-critical productivity inflection points. This is where individual competition becomes counterproductive in the grand scheme of things. By making someone else worse off, the net gains of competitive behaviour are at risk of being neutralised on the collective level. Such behaviour, at a systemic level, doesn't create maximum value. Rather, it preoccupies itself with channelling value to individuals and sacrificing some opportunity for fair mutual gain. It happens largely out of fear and expectation that this is the best way to meet one's own interests. Disastrously, it has led humanity astray countless times.

Most ironically, this incongruous decade-by-decade decline in productivity growth may actually drive us to pursue economic growth even more aggressively. Generally speaking, such a flattening curve in productivity gains is akin to a technology reaching maturity and eventual obsolescence. Take the combustion engine, for instance. It has a limit to how efficient or productive it can optimally be, which is based on the laws of physics as we know it. The same also applies to how cleanly it can burn fuel. Whilst we have seen massive improvements both in fuel consumption and emissions of internal combustion engines over the past several decades, those improvements are harder and harder to come by. Most of us accept that, unless there's a breakthrough innovation that would cause internal combustion technology to leap forward, it is likely reaching its natural limitations. But let's say we were able to make such a leap; this would mean some aspect about the technology would have to change profoundly. As long as the core aspects to the system remain the same, so will the results.

Interestingly, in the case of diesel engines, a breakthrough suddenly appeared on the horizon: researchers had discovered how to develop a newer, much cleaner type of diesel fuel with the promising outlook of reducing CO_2 emissions by about 65% compared to the same quantity of regular diesel fuel. Considering much of the world relies on diesel for transporting goods, this would seem like a rather revolutionary improvement which could help us achieve a massive greenhouse gas emission reduction even before we shift all of our mobility to new propulsion methods. But guess what? The environmental authority in charge decided to deny it a licence under the premise that investment in legacy fuels was a waste of time. This is one example of human self-sabotage caused by narrow-mindedness. The only thing to save the productivity decline in our global economic system is a new and better fuel. Humanity will stand to benefit greatly once we expose individual competition as a sore loser to collaboration. We can only hope the false prophets who keep it alive will overcome their fears of others and wake up to the truth.

Imagine several people with a rope. Each tie their ropes together at one end and then pull on the other end in whichever direction they prefer. Net movement is likely to be minimal. The more frantic and sudden the effort, the more this holds true. I refer to it as competing vector dynamics. The aggregate movement here may end up being far less than the sum of its part – because individuals inadvertently cancel each other out and waste collective resources. This is counterproductive, but when you ask the people involved, you'd likely hear each blame everyone else for the situation. This effect hits us especially hard in times of heightened challenge. *Especially* during times of crisis, self-interest loses out to a focus on shared outcomes and mutual gains.

A recent Harvard University study cited in the *HBR* investigated the effect of collaborative knowledge-sharing on the performance of partners in a law firm during the 2008 financial crisis.[13] They discovered that partners with the most collaborative work style outperformed their peers with their revenue increasing from prior to the crisis. Conversely, those with the least collaborative work style experienced a sharp decline in revenue which they hadn't fully recovered even five years post-crisis.[14] This inevitably means that some of the most highly competitive organisations may not survive our current, or subsequent, crises. Their people choose to trust only themselves, failing to create common ground with others to achieve more together and sustainably. Given that an organisation is created so that groups of people can work together, it seems self-sabotaging that so many have gone down a rabbit hole of excessive, selfish competition, and ultimately lost sight of what really matters. Calling this organisational politics legitimises the thing, whereas it is in fact dangerously counter-productive.

This term alone should make us flinch, given politics are the way we refer to aggregate acts of governance in society. This semantic relationship between the way commercial organisations and governments are described is by no means accidental. The only difference is that being referred to as a leading politician in a corporation is hardly a form of praise, whereas in the context of governments, it often appears to make you a hero of the people. Campaigning of any kind easily derails into selfish pursuits thinly disguised as an altruistic crusade for the greater good. It's like your CEO telling you that taking yet another compliance training is in the best interest of everyone in the company when in reality people can't be motivated otherwise to do what is 'right'.

With a common goal, shared trust and 'we' over the 'I', the frictions we so hate would all but disappear. This clearly affirms that in scenarios and contexts other than the friendly one-on-one competition we sometimes encounter in sportive settings, individual competition has crippling effects on problem-solving, teamwork, productivity, and, most of all, humanity. So why does much of the world still believe in it so fiercely? Let's be honest – how could an economic ideology based on the premise of winners and losers ever lead to collective well-being, prosperity, and satisfaction? Unless we challenge this persistent illusion, global inequality will thrive indefinitely. Trust-enabled collaboration must replace revering antagonism without a cause under the guise of 'efficient competition'. It's time to expose such kinds of narratives for what they are: fairy tales without a happy ending.

> Individual competition has crippling effects on problem-solving, teamwork, productivity, and, most of all, humanity.

Welfare and equality of the whole can suffer greatly when competition takes the upper hand, concentrating power and resources within the grasp of few select individuals. Capitalism has a tendency of attracting more of its kind, and this natural effect is hard to keep in check. Wherever policymaking succeeds in curbing this tendency, it often negatively impacts the sunny side of capitalism as well. Ultimately, capital is simply a vehicle for human (commercial) interaction, such that the tendency for inequities to emerge may well be part human nature. Perhaps this tells us that human hunger for growth and certainty isn't merely a phenomenon of modern times. Even during the agricultural revolution, the sacrifices people were willing to make in order to harvest structure and scale were already evident and not too different from what we are experiencing nowadays. It appears as though complex human collaboration naturally comes with undesired side effects. It's probably worth addressing the underlying symptoms if we want to sustainably advance humanity.

Human obsession with growth is a logical leaning because it appears to promote survival. But growth, if it is to be sustainable, must be natural and driven by genuine need. We frequently find this growth built on the precipices of markets, motivated by an organisation's compulsion to survive its own mounting internal frictions. To such extent, the real motivation behind growth often falls short of a worthwhile purpose or proposition worth being proliferated.

Growth may seem like the natural answer to fixing any capitalist problem, but it's a little more complicated than that. In a system tilting towards growth by default, making the case for mitigating its downsides is a tough sell. It's almost as if growth were truly its own answer, forever beckoning more of it. Conveniently, it covers up the inefficiencies of excessive competition. But lasting growth stems from internal transformation, not internal ignorance. Unlocking latent productivity and performance in existing people and resources within an organisation is the most powerful way of future-proofing any business, especially when the seas are rough. This requires doing better, instead of simply doing more.

Imagine two identical boats flooded with water: each with a sailor and a bucket, the same engine, and equal amounts of fuel. Now, imagine these two boats are racing on speed and distance against each other in a straight line. One sailor uses the bucket to remove the water right away, leaving the engine idling until most of the water is gone, then giving it the beans. The other gives the engine full throttle from the get-go, relying solely on the weather and waves to expel water from the boat. How do you think the race will end?

Imagine the same race would be conducted with two sailors per boat. In one boat, both sailors quickly agree to divide and conquer: one sailor handles the engine, monitoring speed and fuel levels to determine the optimum throttle, while the other does their best to remove water from the boat. They know to rely on and trust each other so that they can focus on the task at hand and perform well. Every now and then, they switch positions so that the more strenuous work is shared fairly. On the competing boat, the two sailors first spend considerable time arguing about who is in charge, fighting over who gets which post first and thereafter constantly interfere with each other's duties, believing each knows better than the other.

In direct comparison, the collaborative team significantly outperforms the competitive one. Yet strangely, and perhaps because a yardstick for direct comparison almost never truly exists in the real world, many organisations are stuck in the second scenario without even fully realising its detrimental effect. In this rich metaphor, the water weighing down the boat also represents the transformation challenge that many organisations face. Once overcome, we can recover our speed, agility, and effectiveness. But this is only possible with the right collaboration to begin with. Many people believe change takes effort – but that effort, deployed well, yields results far beyond its initial input. Meanwhile, maintaining a dysfunctional status quo also requires considerable effort. Unfortunately, effort in this scenario is expended on misunderstandings, arguments and blame instead of the actual tasks at hand. Aggressively ambitious growth seems to be the only way out, although that wholly ignores the need and opportunity to solve the underlying problem at hand. Growth, therefore, becomes a strategy for compensating the inefficiencies that be and postponing the removal of dysfunction. This is akin to fixing a leaking vessel by increasing the size of the bucket, instead of plugging the hole. It's a lot like trying to drink from a fork – it doesn't work very well, and it makes you look ridiculous.

Endnotes

1   https://www.ncbi.nlm.nih.gov/pmc/articles/PMC5374256/

2   https://www.researchgate.net/publication/310033638_Parochial_altruism_Pitfalls_and_prospects#pf1e

3   https://scholar.harvard.edu/files/shleifer/files/competition_ethics.pdf

4   https://www.tandfonline.com/doi/abs/10.1080/00207659.2019.1684081

5   https://www.jstor.org/stable/657866

6   https://www.sciencedirect.com/science/article/abs/pii/016726819290050L

7   https://science.sciencemag.org/content/211/4481/453.abstract

8   https://www.researchgate.net/profile/Kendra_Strauss/publication/227464892_Re-Engaging_with_Rationality_in_Economic_Geography_Behavioural_Approaches_and_the_Importance_of_Context_in_Decision-Making/links/5c6ef2a7458515831f650aaf/Re-Engaging-with-Rationality-in-Economic-Geography-Behavioural-Approaches-and-the-Importance-of-Context-in-Decision-Making.pdf

9   https://www.ted.com/talks/dan_pink_the_puzzle_of_motivation/transcript?language=en

10 https://www.ted.com/talks/yves_morieux_how_too_many_rules_at_work_keep_you_from_getting_things_done

11 https://fortune.com/2016/01/28/business-decision-making-project-management/

12 Ibid. https://fortune.com/2016/01/28/business-decision-making-project-management/

13 https://hbr.org/2020/07/7-strategies-for-promoting-collaboration-in-a-crisis

14 https://journals.aom.org/doi/pdf/10.5465/apbpp.2002.7510158

Chapter 3

WHAT GOT US HERE
WON'T GET US THERE

Getting ready for a new operating system

P recisely because human cooperative dynamics are so powerful, we may often find ourselves at their mercy instead of the other way around. The miracle of human collaboration always retains the hope of a brighter future on the horizon, but its actual effects might resemble dark magic more than anything else, luring us into traps we didn't see coming. Our ability to shape our planet and reshape our lives may well track back to a collaboration miracle, but some of this spirit of teamwork has inevitably been disposed of in the process. Distrust is the most likely reason for this. Modern management theory contributed to alienating us from preferring collaboration over competition with a line of reasoning that appears logical, but directly contradicts how we are wired and what made us

> Modern management theory contributed to alienating us from preferring collaboration over competition with a line of reasoning that appears logical, but directly contradicts how we are wired and what made us successful to begin with.

successful to begin with. And this worldview became extremely influential and powerful.

There are more people on this planet than we could have ever imagined. We fixed many problems humanity has faced over the years, but very reliably new problems have emerged. The magic of capital is brilliant and tempting and has got us very far as people, but unfortunately it is also conflicting with the magic of humanity that is at the core of our being. There are many reasons for why you might feel that there is something missing in this incredible world we have created.

As such, this means much brainpower has been devoted to less-than-ideal pursuits. The 2008 Financial Crisis, for instance, crystallised the damaging effects of overindulgence in our global financial system with some estimating the true cost of government bailouts alone close to $500 billion.[1] In part, this can be attributed to an irrational culture of exuberance in financial institutions and society at the time (and perhaps even more so today).[2,3]

My explanation rests on financial institutions' hyper-competitive and highly regulated environments fuelling a supercharged form of selfishness among individual actors who narrowly trusted their own abilities and, therefore, made distrust of others the norm. In their crusades, they did make a killing – but it eventually killed the entire system. Since it's entirely impossible to cooperate with someone you distrust, the focus wasn't on enlarging the pie; it was on enrichment at any cost. This is presumably because the regulation and systems in place to govern financial markets couldn't check such behaviour no matter how hard they tried. When we forget about the bigger picture, systems we build can become vehicles of wrongful conduct with the guise of a clean conscience. The selfishness of speculators leading up to the Financial Crisis brought with it large-scale doom.

But far from all corrective impulses come to us as large-scale worldwide crises. Many disruptions we deal with occur more frequently, unfold more slowly, and cover a specific industry or context. We often refer to those as disruptive shifts: digital cameras, cloud computing and social media to name a few. What all have in common beyond this is a shared pattern – a pattern revealing a deeper truth about the world we live in and the ever-changing goalposts of what it takes to succeed in it. Trust, as will become apparent throughout this book, is a pivotal element of this pattern. But disruption would be too narrow of a concept to truly understand change. Most change actually takes an evolutionary path in its totality, with jolts of disruption along the way for innovation professors to feast on. Like that symbolic frog sitting in a casserole being heated, we often realise big changes once they have already come into fruition, which is why they can feel like an ambush. Disruption exists only in the sense that we fail to see what's coming. Much of the picture reveals itself after the fact – at a point when there is no going back. These disruptive

> Disruption exists only in the sense that we fail to see what's coming. Much of the picture reveals itself after the fact – at a point when there is no going back.

shifts over the decades, made possible by advances in technology, have largely exerted influence on human behaviour.

We've never had a greater ability to connect with more people in more ways than we do now. This has happened both at the transactional and relational level, and those two dimensions of increasing interconnection have coexisted for some time. The corporate world especially has continued to lean on a pre-dominantly transactional modus operandi – perhaps more than we would like. In many organisations, social capital is often penalised because it is deemed a conflict of interest. This is the problem with the compliance model that exists in most modern organisations and institutions today. It is counter-intuitive to human nature. A more effective compliance regime requires individual proactiveness and care. If there is one thing that humans have proven since they have formed civilisations, it is our ability regulate behaviour amongst ourselves – so long as we are given permission and trust to do so.

The sharing economy – which I call the *Trust Economy* – has shown us that this form of community or self-regulation works extremely well especially when facilitated by technology. It's the blueprint for a world more compatible with our collaborative and relational human nature. So far, that world at best coexists with the transactional status quo. Paradoxically, whilst both have completely divergent priorities, they would actually complement each other. For instance, the informal network of relationships in organisations often directly contradicts formal structures put in place – but if both were aligned, everyone would benefit. This applies equally to the economy at whole: We must merge the transaction economy with the *Trust Economy*, instead of having the two coexist and conflict. It's just unfortunate that many people still don't see what's wrong with the way things have always been – and thus won't understand why disruptive shifts are going to be happening to begin with.

In his book *False Prophets*, Jim Hoopes examines the legacy of influential early management thinkers (of which Adam Smith was but one recognisable name) and its detriment to social and economic harmony. He observes that we tend to have a love-hate relationship with corporate life. Corporations may have given us access to things we didn't have at our disposal in the past, but they have not necessarily empowered us in the process.

Until this day, the business of management gurus is thriving precisely because our relationship with corporate reality is one of ambivalence and interdependence. But rarely do the thinkers challenging the status quo also tackle its foundations. Hardly ever does a management theory question the existence of the corporation to begin with. *The Trust Economy* demonstrates that human collaboration can be largely liberated from reliance on the traditional corporate form factor. Organisations could become organisms, liberated from the shackles of static systems and avalanches of complexity, enabling them to then become driven by an agility-driven culture focused on solving problems instead of drowning them in a cement pile of administration.

People like Hoopes didn't become contrarians by necessity, but by choice. The world needs people who point out the obvious whenever it's hiding in plain sight.

For instance, you may be wondering why a global pandemic prompted a toilet paper shortage in many places around the world.

As social creatures, our actions must always be understood in the social context in which they occur, which we have previously implored. The systems and realities we have created for ourselves shape that context. As a result, our behaviour adjusts in bizarre ways.

Enter that infamous Adam Smith quote from 1776 on the 'invisible hand': *"It is not from the benevolence of the butcher, the brewer, or the baker that we expect our dinner, but from their regard to their own self-interest. We address ourselves not to their humanity but to their self-love, and never talk to them of our own necessities, but of their advantages"* (Adam Smith, *Wealth of Nations*, Vol 1). Since then, the world of business has sponged up and internalised this mantra far more than is healthy for anyone involved. This assumption of self-interest was essentially flawed, but the powerful picture it created is but one example of how human minds derail into biases that harm rather than help.

Does that mean humanity shot itself in the foot by embracing industrialisation? Where anti-industrialists and their counterparts produce compelling narratives in favour of each extreme, the only truly relevant questions to ask in a world already defined by industrial (infra-) structure must focus on how we can transform it for the better: by transforming to a more human-centred philosophy surrounding it.

What it also requires is ridding ourselves of prejudice around human behaviour, particularly the firm belief that humans are naturally untrustworthy, or that appealing to individual selfishness can lead to collective prosperity and a happy ever after. It necessitates careful examination of the legacy belief systems surviving in management practices until this day – systems which

Hoopes identifies as thoroughly undemocratic and inextricably linked to the age of slavery, tracing origins to 'management manuals' used by slave-drivers. Most certainly, these tools were not geared towards finding purpose, engagement, and mutual trust – and, where they continue to be in place, their burden exists with them. Adam Smith didn't see himself as a slave driver – but in shaping our industrial-economic thinking and its eponymous complex, he was one of the false prophets who enslaved us to the rat race by making it sound like a cheese party.

Smith was somewhat right in asserting that mutual self-interest could achieve collective gain (this is the core economic argument for why humans benefit from trade), but he colours his observations with undue judgements of human nature. Smith believed that people's natural tendency toward selfishness drove the 'invisible hand'. But people's behaviour is largely incongruent with this assumption. As we've discussed previously, we prioritise collective interest (cooperation) when dealing with members of the same social group or 'tribe' as opposed to aggression and competition (self-preservation) when facing aliens.

Even if we ignore that, however, Smith's postulation is not reflective of reality. In Smith's time, it was in fact extremely common to have a personal and cordial relationship with one's butcher, baker, and brewer. Just like some of us practice today, such interactions were founded on shared social capital and strong bonds of mutual trust and respect. The interest of each party in maintaining the relationship with the other was the source from which each could satisfy their self-interest. Smith wasn't just plain wrong; his judgement of the human character managed to poison our perspective on economic interactions for centuries to come.

In fact, Smith's words align to an anonymous, dehumanised global capitalism causing much environmental, social, and moral damage in our world. Before we smith this argument into a blame game aimed at our industrial history, it's worth highlighting that Adam Smith all but propelled forth a concept that had shaped humanity since the arrival of agriculture: a static system governance over the agile system governance that probably defined hunter-gatherer living. Before the advent of technology as we know it, agility simply couldn't scale. Collaboration systems that enabled us to transact at scale were a good idea, except for the spill-over influence on how we *interact*. The great news for us is that with the end of industrial revolution, fewer of our fellow humans are fraught with working 18-hour shifts in polluted factories (although perhaps not as few as we would like). It means many of us can afford to move past industrial thinking.

Social hierarchies were always part of human (and other primate) life. The natural formation of social hierarchies in human communities appears to have offered more advantages than drawbacks. This may change once communities are formalised in systems co-existing (or even conflicting) with these natural hierarchies.[4] An entry level employee in a big corporation has little formal status in the corporate hierarchy but might carry high status as a striker in their local soccer club. We often find formal and informal hierarchies in direct conflict with each other, raising the question of which will prevail in reality. The more both are out of sync the more challenging and perhaps frustrating human interactions around them become. If you have ever observed a fellow human trying to unsuccessfully impress their chosen target with their job or wealth, you have seen this principle in action. Navigating between contexts and the implicit and explicit status dynamics and pecking orders within and between each can be exhausting and confusing. Understanding our role within our social fabric is important, and increasingly difficult in a complex global world.

What makes matters even more puzzling is the increasing hierarchical distance afforded by formal systems. Perhaps a tribal leader in a group of foragers had the greatest access to mating partners, but they probably did not have 100 or 1,000 times more than the lowest status individual. This is because the collaborative nature of humanity would want to prevent extreme inequality so long as reciprocal relationships are in the foreground. The industrialisation of the world and the globalisation that followed, together with money as arguably our most versatile kind of capital, has turned our attention away from looking after each other. And with this, we look towards a promise that by merely transacting with each other, everybody would be adequately taken care of. In reality, we haven't really taken care of our fellow people and even less so the environment upon which we all depend. It's because a transactional mindset means that we don't have to care about those we do business with, as long as we universally care about the monetary gains inherent in the activity – which is a pretty sobering thought.

When human foragers started communicating with language, not only did they build the foundation for uniquely human collaboration, they also moved towards a more egalitarian social model.[5] Status was a means for maintaining order, and not an end in itself to be glorified and worshipped. It goes without saying that such a society built on minimum viable inequity was a more fruitful place than one built on maximum viable bragging.

Social status and money have overshadowed the far more fruitful and inclusive concepts of collaboration and capital enabled by relationships. The magic of capital and relationships should obviously serve to create a sum greater than its individual parts. The way we look at capital and relationships for the most part nowadays has replaced that win-win situation with one in which we compete for resources and divide rather than share. This catapults us right back on the same playing field with other primates. That is definitely not where we belong.

In *The Trust Economy*, I made a point very close to my heart.[6] I established that we are inclined to trust the people around us. Trust makes us happy and maximises the effectiveness of our collaboration and coexistence. The irony is that the systems we ended up building around that very collaboration and coexistence ended up encouraging exactly the opposite. Modern cities and societies are built on the principle of mutual distrust. This is why we have locks, rules, and penalties. The problem with that is that it doesn't actually make us happy. It may have enabled economic growth in social health but hasn't been nearly as effective in achieving what actually and truly matters to us, which is human happiness. It has also made it difficult to maintain any wide-ranging form of social equity. This means that in societies where rules are put above all else, there is no escaping inequality. When people have an understanding, rules

> When people have an understanding, rules should be a formality at best — because a common denominator matters more.

should be a formality at best – because a common denominator matters more.

In reality, cooperation is only the case between the parties to a trade. In the bigger scheme of things, people compete for these trades to happen. For instance, if you are a blueberry farmer in Chile looking to sell to a wholesaler in Asia, the sale of your blueberries in exchange for cash is technically a win-win situation. You prefer to receive money in exchange for your blueberries, and the wholesaler prefers to receive your blueberries instead of sticking to their cash because they intend to sell them and realise a profit from this activity. But looking at a trade in isolation like this is unrealistic; both the wholesaler and the blueberry farmer have other options. The most immediate consideration is doing business with another counterparty. This means that a trade, which is in itself cooperative, exists in the context of a competitive environment. To further complicate matters, the power imbalance between parties to a trade is usually unequal. This means that one party has more options, leverage and, therefore, a clear advantage over the other. While both parties stand to gain from the transaction, one is likely to gain more.

There are many reasons for this inequity; ignoring it and focusing only on the purported win-win nature of trade is a rational idea but counter-intuitive to our nature. Humans have a natural tendency towards reciprocal behaviour, and the outcome of such reciprocity is supposed to be equal gain on both sides. In the case of social capital, where the gains cannot be quantified because they may not involve money, the default assumption is that the gains on both sides are roughly equal. This means both parties can maintain that they have treated each other fairly, which is likely to strengthen their relationship.

In the case of global trade, we are looking at a far more transactional interaction, at least when we look at the transactions themselves. Of course, relationships are a pivotal dimension of doing business around the world, but their relevance is often tagged to the context and nature of transactions taking place between individuals involved. The problem is that even the best relationships in this realm cannot guarantee equal distribution of gains across the value chain. This reality has enabled the flow of value in a particular direction, leading to the concentration of value and power in the hands of a select few. This, in turn, intensifies the competition amongst those who receive the shorter end of the stick. When human nature tells us to value each other's contributions in such a way that we achieve equity, the way we trade tells the opposite story – a story in which some stand to gain more than others.

Our universal focus on money has led to its emergence as the most valuable thing we have, and correspondingly incited a fierce competition for it. With a global emphasis on transactional interaction and competition, we have actually eroded much of the magic of collaboration that made humanity great in the first place. The upside to this is that we can do business with people we neither like nor trust because the common ground we share is money. But the downside is: competition is vastly less effective and value-generating than cooperation, meaning that in the grand scheme of things, we actually end up with less

> With a global emphasis on transactional interaction and competition, we have actually eroded much of the magic of collaboration that made humanity great in the first place.

value than if we were to collaborate. Competition is a zero-sum game. We legitimise short-sighted selfishness, even though it compromises the whole for all of us. This is the kind of mindset that results from making people believe that it's okay to not care about those they trade with. In the early days of humanity, that selfishness would have likely been short-lived. But thanks to the way our societies operate today, we keep it alive with the effect of accidentally contaminating our supposedly collaborative economic interactions with others.

Selfishness is not one of the traits commonly quoted in happiness research. There's no hiding that we created a world for ourselves in which it is easier than ever before to be miserable and feel like that's an accomplishment. It's time we press that inner *RESET* button and remind our brains and fellow humans that we are actually engineered to do things differently. The more we fight our own battles, the less capable we will become of progressing humanity overall. Progress is a positive sum game by definition. If you take from one part of the world and use it to enrich another, what's the net progress for our planet? Our 'me'-centric culture needs to be replaced with something making us better off both individually and collectively. We must bring back the idea of reciprocity into the way we exchange goods, services, and value. In an equal relationship, it is much more difficult for you to squeeze the other party on things like price or make them agree to a deal skewed in your favour. You actually care about the other person.

Endnotes

1 https://mitsloan.mit.edu/ideas-made-to-matter/heres-how-much-2008-bailouts-really-cost

2 https://insights.som.yale.edu/insights/did-culture-cause-the-financial-crisis

3   https://www.tandfonline.com/doi/abs/10.1080/17530350.2012.703143
4   https://www.journals.uchicago.edu/doi/abs/10.1086/341744
5   https://www.sciencedirect.com/science/article/pii/S2405844017320996
6   https://www.amazon.com/Trust-Economy-Building-Realising-Exponential/dp/9814751669

Chapter 4

WE'RE IN THIS TOGETHER
Discovering a better globalism

The more complex the world became, the more we readily abandoned relationships for transactions as a means of getting by. Interacting with vastly more people forced us to formalise our interactions and ensure they are adequately supported by systems to maintain an overview of what was going on. A mass market fuelled by money simply wasn't compatible with a relationship-first approach. Our reliance on capital and technology became more than a modus operandi. It turned into a faith in itself – and a persistently universal one at that.

> Our reliance on capital and technology became more than a modus operandi. It turned into a faith in itself – and a persistently universal one at that.

The growth prompted by this system of transaction improved our living conditions over time. With efficiency optimised, at the consequence of all else being compromised, people had more free time at their disposal. The systematisation of our world also brought other benefits with it, such as an infrastructural renaissance to the critical building blocks of our society like medical services. Most of this ensued from collective understanding that advancements in our healthcare systems were a necessary ingredient for sustaining economic growth.[1] However, the drawbacks to our rapid development have been apparent for decades. Its adverse effects on the planet and humanity were as much a relevant topic of discussion a half a century ago as today.[2]

Academics and intellectuals have questioned the actual merits of the economic growth and capital fixation defining most contemporary human environments. Take the Easterlin Paradox. Coined by Richard Easterlin in 1974, it states that as incomes continue to rise over time, happiness does not increase in the same way.[3] Other studies somewhat logically conclude growth achieved at the price of *rising inequality* also does not translate to overall increases in happiness.[4] So why do we continue to put up with it?

The reason is likely simple. As one article finds, happiness *does* rise with income *in the short-term*, but this effect is offset in the long run.[5] In addition, as economic standards rise, so do people's expectations.[6] This means that economic growth, however much of a cure-all it seems, does not necessarily help humanity reach its ultimate pursuit, let alone solve its pressing problems. This should make us re-evaluate the merits of our fixation on growth, especially its role as a silver bullet solution to everything, from revitalising a region to world peace. Akin to painting a rusty fence, this is only insofar a good idea as you have the resources and gumption to keep painting, even if proper sanding and restoration would pay much greater dividends in the end.

Now let's return to our friendly foe, Adam Smith, for a moment. By dangling the legitimation of absolute selfishness (for the greater good!) in front of us, the likes of Adam Smith lured us with the ultimate temptation: the idea that we should stop caring about the rest of the world and take what's ours, better still, doing so with a clean conscience. Like a proverbial snake tempting us to pluck the apple from the forbidden tree, theories like the *invisible hand* were trustworthy and compelling enough for us to abandon basic human intuition in their favour. The idea was that self-interested actions in a free market (i.e., freedom of production and consumption) would balance supply with demand and inevitably lead to fulfilment of society's best interests. When it comes to trade, this idea holds in principle. Trade requires both sides to gain from a transaction. But Smith was wrong about his theory of selfishness as the underlying principle that makes us all better off. Competition is such a tempting idea because it appears to make us better off in the short term. Win-lose thinking gives us instant gratification and all too easily makes us forget that the sum of collaboration is always greater.

Quintessentially, our obsession with economic growth and capital has perhaps become addictive to the extent that it no longer serves our purposes. What began as an ingenious system for mass collaboration transformed into an uncontrollable rebranding of

> What began as an ingenious system for mass collaboration transformed into an uncontrollable rebranding of selfishness as altruism and, to the same effect, greed as efficiency.

selfishness as altruism and, to the same effect, greed as efficiency. It has given humanity the ultimate excuse to not care about anyone but themselves because *'the markets will take care of the rest'.* In countries with well-developed public social support systems, that narrative has been somewhat modified to *'the government will take care of the rest'.* Many of the behaviours we consider normal in purely transactional economic dealings would be completely unacceptable were we to behave in such ways towards our friends. For instance, you might treat a rental vehicle differently than your friend's car that you borrowed for a weekend. Why? Because you *care* about your friend, and your relationship with them. Now, imagine all of the collective unpleasantry between people transacting within the socio-economic systems governing us. Also imagine how different the world would look like if we made the effort to behave towards everyone as we would towards our friend and their car. Why would we want to juggle such a two-faced existence between our economic and social selves, when collaborating with others makes

> Many of the behaviours we consider normal in purely transactional economic dealings would be completely unacceptable were we to behave in such ways towards our friends.

us happier and better off in all aspects of life? Wouldn't it be a much better strategy to *make the world a better place by invigorating relationships, good behaviour, reciprocal kindness, and mutual trust* than yet another effort to *stimulate growth and competition, scepticism, and hostility*? How much of a cynic do you have to be to believe that is a more effective approach? How do you think subscribing to it has damaged humanity?

Our reciprocal social disposition naturally protects us from grave inequality and misery, at least in theory. But that very nature is compromised by a religious pursuit of selfish motives which are a lure for our own and humanity's perpetual suffering and demise. As one of the most intriguing studies on human altruism aptly finds, selfishness of a few can derail a beautiful interdependent collaboration system:

> *"Experimental evidence indicates that human altruism is a powerful force and is unique in the animal world. However, there is much individual heterogeneity and the interaction between altruists and selfish individuals is vital to human cooperation. Depending on the environment, a minority of altruists can force a majority of selfish individuals to cooperate or, conversely, a few egoists can induce a large number of altruists to defect."*[7]

Perhaps all we need to do is rid ourselves of our wishful belief in the benevolence of selfishness, our blasphemous worship of money, and our addiction to short-term thinking and its illusory promise of lasting happiness. Such obsessions are the socio-economic equivalent of fast-food addiction: you visibly gain immediately, but if you're honest with yourself, it doesn't make you feel too good – and it eventually makes you sick.

This matters because the collaboration systems we created to work better together have been developed to such an extent that they started working against us. The cause is likely due to the fact that, at some point in the process, we lost sight that many of the systems we created were simply means to help us collaborate in the best possible way. But because all human systems are ultimately extensions of our culture, and accordingly regulate how we think and behave, they acquired symbolic relevance as a by-product of their use. We nowadays think that it's a more than appropriate deal to perceive the means to human collaboration as ends in themselves. For instance, modern society delights in speaking about and glorifying social and economic status and its associated symbolism – but more often than not, we use it to distance ourselves from other people.

Take job titles, for instance. They help people understand what we and others do at work. But in reality, these titles are indicators of pecking order more than anything else. In many corporations, job titles aren't just lengthy and semantically bizarre, but also add to the confusion of what a person's job instead of helping understand precisely that. More so, they come in handy as giving people legitimate excuses for what *isn't* their job. In an organisation where the declared objective is the collective achievement of a mission, vision, or purpose, this *shouldn't* matter. It should be natural for everyone to do what's needed so that the organisation can thrive. But that isn't how modern bureaucracy works. Modern bureaucracy, in many cases, *doesn't* work, and job titles illustrate this perfectly.

Due to the mind-boggling complexity of modern organisations, titles may have nothing to do with the mandate or remuneration of an individual, let alone their implied competency. Can you, for instance, tell the difference between a local branch senior assistant vice president, a vice president working for a country business and the regional cluster assistant vice president? Many titles also include secondary descriptors, which are supposedly reflective of a person's work responsibilities. In that case, it may strike you that having several *levels* of chief digital officers, several heads of innovation, and various transformation officers might lead to uncertainty that actually stands in the way of changing a business for the better. Much of this happens due to individual initiative that, more often than not, takes place in a corporate vacuum. If title mumbo-jumbo like this doesn't confuse you, you're either all too accustomed to corporate environments or, as perhaps a converse result thereof, you simply ignore these titles altogether. It's but one real-world example of the meaningless jungle that gets in the way of work actually being done.

The pertinent question then becomes: why do we keep these relatively useless relics in place? Why don't we do something to counteract the mounting complexity inside organisations before it grinds us to a halt? The pathological proliferation of complexity is a reality in most modern organisations and a direct result of the way in which we have built them – not, as we'd like to tell ourselves, a *fact of life*. This is partly caused by our tendency to try putting every person and their job in a box because that apparently helps with *management and accountability*. Titles often identify corporate tribes by *division* when they could and should instead focus on common ground and shared purpose. Because people are not robots, this can lead to various frictions and hostilities, even if through passive transgressions. This is why industry incumbents are dramatically less effective than competing technology disruptors that are making headway into some of these established markets. The agility that many young companies naturally have at their disposal and their often sharper focus on building a winning customer value proposition affords them a significant edge, simply because they run a different operating system. What they mostly lack is legacy. In lieu of it they may have greater chaos, but equally they benefit from an often leaner, technology-enabled administration. It may sound like a minute detail, but the crucial difference between both operations is that technology is far more flexible and scalable than static, paper-derived classic administration approaches could ever amount to be. Technology enables companies to be far better at handling the complexity of our world today, especially those without decades of operational baggage. That, and only that, is why technology may be eating the world, as some Silicon Valley prophets like to righteously remark.

Don't for a moment believe, however, that start-ups and the new economy are allergic or immune to titles, politics, and excessive competition. Quite the opposite. Whilst a young company with a sophisticated technology infrastructure may have innate potential to be very agile, it will still need a company culture that enables it. Conversely, even an organisation with significant amounts of bureaucracy of the traditional variety can be highly effective with the right cultural foundations in place. This is why culture is proverbially said to eat strategy (and structure) for breakfast (lunch, and dinner). Technology is highly useful as an enabler and amplifier augmenting what we do, but not as a solution itself. Technology is neither good nor bad, but neutral; it's all in what we do with it. You can have the best, most expensive and latest generation skiing equipment in the world, but you still wouldn't stand a chance of beating the world ski jumping champion at their own game. Experience is useful without equipment; the opposite doesn't necessarily hold true. Connecting this to titles, they are essentially labels for our human equipment. And they are truly just that. In Italy, you occasionally spot a Fiat 500 sporting a generously dimensioned Ferrari badge. Whether you call that ambition or deceit is up to you, but what I do know is people with Ferrari titles do not always live up to corresponding expectations. Titles give us an excuse to make assumptions purely based on the expectations of the label, when we should be reading the situation presenting itself. If you drive a hatchback and put a Ferrari sticker on the front, does it really change what's on the inside? I'm not saying titles are evil or that nobody lives up to them, but rather that they can be more distracting than they are helpful. A title doesn't *actually* tell you whether somebody is capable of doing anything for you. It's a shortcut that, like all labels, should never prevail over common sense.

Organisations must stop focusing on polishing formal aspects of their structure and redirect their energy towards their role as a means to an end for their stakeholders. This prevents them from further glorifying the means and forgetting all about the end they were supposed to achieve. In a truly effective environment, outcomes matter much more than how those outcomes are attained, because we can trust the people involved to find an adequate and ethical means to the end. This is a better approach to maximising the outputs of those working with you because the gains are based on their own devices, not the labels and boxes that you devise for them. This is true for every system that humanity ever constructed and explains why it's hard to shift from existing systems to new ones: status quo legacy has become habit and therefore become part of us. The more we accelerated human progress, the more rapidly collaboration systems created by us became technically obsolete, even though practically we continued relying on them as per the usual. Many legacy ways of doing things that once made sense but are now a burden have become deeply ingrained in our thinking, which means they follow us far beyond their useful life span. Often, we realise just how peculiar they really are once we finally question their *raison d'être*.

This illustrates how our ingenuity and the magic by which we collaborate eventually turns on us. It shows why our technological progress has been exponential, whilst our capacity to leverage that technology in the form of elevated productivity and well-being continues to be limited. Well-trodden paths established by what we relied on in the past are so enigmatic in our thinking that they have remained with us irrespective of their actual *objective* utility today. This is the story of convention getting in the way of change, and it's particularly difficult to draw the line between what's worth keeping and what needs to go. That might explain why many people elect to maintain a safe distance from change initiatives altogether.

> Well-trodden paths established by what we relied on in the past are so enigmatic in our thinking that they have remained with us irrespective of their actual *objective* utility today.

To this effect, globalism must deviate from such a legacy-driven approach. The key is to understand how we've been shaped by our past success and how it may stand in the way of future progress. In some common law countries, for instance, wearing wigs in court was still mandatory until very recently. No further explanation is needed to illustrate how such legacies might be obsolete – although it can be entertaining to ponder over their long-standing existence.

When you take a closer look at your everyday environment, you will be able to excavate an indefinite number of these rich fossils symbolising solutions that once proved to be useful, but long outlived their utility and yet remain ever-present in society today. You may also realise how much they have become intertwined with our culture we hold dearly. For example, your grandmother may consider it foolish of you to *innovate* her tried and tested recipes. Depending on the kind of grandma you have, she might even find it disrespectful or offensive. She may also have a point, considering her outstanding expertise on the subject matter. In that sense, grandma's recipes are the little sister of *'but this is how we've always done it'* thinking in business. Depending on the objective quality of what is being created and its relevance in the world that we exist in today, thinking along such lines may preserve or harm our success. It really *depends*. Not all innovation is intelligent, and not all efforts at preservation are worth it. Overall, our questioning and willingness to experiment may help us distinguish grandma's world-famous apple pie from that pasta dish only your family likes. Grandma was probably right about her recipes, but many executives yielding to the temptations of such thinking have been proven dead wrong, and so were the companies they spearheaded.

The lines between conventions that have outlived their useful life and those carrying important nostalgic and cultural value worth preserving are blurred at best. It is the role of change-makers to tell them apart. When we take a step back and look at the myriad of human legacy systems with fresh perspective, new pathways reveal themselves. Sometimes it takes a catalyst to awaken us from a slumber and confront the status quo *for what it is*. Making a distinction between what is worth retiring and what we should be keeping is best achieved by looking at outcomes. Our new take on globalism will have to transition from a focus on status quo form factors to a focus on meaningful outcomes. You could argue that human trade and collaboration are simply a means to an end – to minimise harm and maximise happiness at individual and collective levels. Once we realise that focusing on what we actually want (i.e., the purpose behind what we do and how we interact with each other) is a more effective strategy than organising our thinking around worship of existing systems and conventions, we will most likely be happier for it.

Endnotes

1   https://www.sciencedirect.com/science/article/pii/S1098301512041526

2   https://search.proquest.com/openview/6ce2d5a919778d8fada2059d39b7f f89/1?pq-origsite=gscholar&cbl=1817076

3   https://www.sciencedirect.com/science/article/pii/B9780122050503500087

4   https://journals.sagepub.com/doi/abs/10.1177/0956797615596713

5   https://www.ncbi.nlm.nih.gov/pmc/articles/PMC3012515/

6   https://www.sciencedirect.com/science/article/abs/pii/016726819500003B

7   https://www.nature.com/articles/nature02043

the new global

‘The problem with having everything is, you run out of ideas for how to buy happiness. ’

Chapter 5

SOCIAL CAPITAL(-ISM)
The human currency

Human society is impossible to maintain in the absence of trust. Nations, governments, and corporations exist only in the human imagination. Our collective trust in their existence makes them real. Have a monkey choose between a banana and an Apple Inc. share, and you see this in action. The same applies to money – another figment of the human imagination that relies on our collective trust. It's ironic that something like money, which frequently causes people to distrust each other, relies on mutual and shared trust in order to even exist. Once trust leaves the monetary system, value naturally leaves with it. Inflation and bank runs devalue currencies;

> It's ironic that something like money, which frequently causes people to distrust each other, relies on mutual and shared trust in order to even exist.

scandals devalue stock prices; forgery devalues goods and services. Without trust, currencies, companies, stocks, and relationships are close to worthless. Money is our most universal system of value, and also the ultimate trust intermediary between people. We might not trust each other, but we mutually trust money. This transaction-level consensus allows us to do business with people we don't know or like.

But it also clashes with our hard-wired nature as social creatures. By removing the role of relationships and interpersonal trust, money has caused us equal pain as it brought gain. Many societies and organisations have seen exceptional economic growth in the past several decades, yet the human condition hasn't necessarily improved with it. Economic growth tends to increase inequality – particularly in countries that are in a relatively less privileged position in the first place.[1] Money has never been a humane or relational currency; it is, by definition, transactional. What makes money superior to barter is its liquidity, but as *time banks* have shown, social capital alternatives to fiat currency can work at a community level. *Time banks* essentially provide a means of accounting for social capital in the form of recording and repurposing it into a currency of hours people earn availing their expertise and services to others. It's a circular economy approach, which works on the assumption that an entire community gains from helping each other reciprocally. By using the quantum of time, this model is naturally inclusive since everyone has the same absolute quantity available in a day. *Time banking* has been argued to positively impact communities.[2] Its principles are the same as for all social capital interactions; they are mutual and reciprocal, and they naturally gravitate towards an equilibrium in which the gains are collectively enjoyed.

Further enhanced by digital possibilities, we are reaching a point where socially conscious alternatives to money can be effectively used *at scale*, in some cases even replacing the need for certain money transactions. Such social capital transactions are much more relational in nature, and often require a certain level of interpersonal trust to exist. When they are facilitated by digital platforms like the ones many of us use daily, trust-building and the economic transactions and interactions that follow can be a frictionless and rewarding experience. Their integration of monetary and social capital makes them highly effective collaboration instruments; we typically refer to this as the sharing economy, or as I like to call it, the *Trust Economy*. I'm speaking about a form of economic interaction which we might call social capitalism. Community and connection are at the heart of it.

It's not surprising that many tech companies and start-ups make prolific use of the term *community* in relation to their propositions. Communities always matter to people. Not much has changed about this or about their nature in centuries – other than how we discover and connect with them. Communities are usually built on a shared belief system, typically aim to grow in size, rely on a (formal or informal) code of conduct, and, accordingly, manifest their very own subculture or identity.

Communities are movements proliferated by passionate evangelists promoting their merits. Nowadays our access to communities is far more global and easier than in the past, leading to the formation of global affinity clusters with people from all walks of life and corners of the earth. Such a collaborative cloud of people assembling around a common

> Communities are movements proliferated by passionate evangelists promoting their merits.

cause is hardly different from groups of people congregating around fireplaces in the good old times. Both contexts are environments for stories to be shared and mutual support to be extended. These associations provide a refuge for people and, depending on their nature, can also establish platforms of positive change. Anything from a social network to a professional body, your local church or your neighbour's book club broadly fall within this definition. Communities form the heart of the emerging social capitalism we are seeing gain momentum around the world. They enrich us on professional and personal levels because they focus on the mutual shared benefit obtained by all those involved.

Interestingly, until today, human capacity to *self-organise* is limited to relatively small group sizes – so long as the effort is done purely informally. This is why we simply *had to* adopt systems and structures that would allow us to grow our trade networks beyond natural limits like these. It's also why the formation of cities and economies as we know today became possible. Communities are becoming ever more prolific and serve an important role in balancing increasingly hostile and overbureaucratised administrative and corporate environs. The bridges they build are invaluable in equalising competitive behaviours in and across organisations, in that they remind us of shared causes worth caring about. You can regard them as a gentle but effective antidote to the global distrust epidemic that has been unfolding before our eyes for quite some time. The proliferation of digital communities and their ability to scale effortlessly with the help of technology reemphasised relationship-driven business practices in which the transaction is a means to a human end, rather than the other way around.

In reinventing our corporate and economic interactions, technology has also, in many places, naturally augmented transactions with community and relationship aspects, reintroducing a sense of humanity to the act of exchanging value with strangers. It means people now have a much more immediate opportunity to build a social and professional network alongside their economic consumption, which is better than these two dimensions of our lives arbitrarily coexisting. This probably did not happen by accident, but simply reflects our natural preference towards connecting on common ground.

It also compounded the trend toward a relationship renaissance in the business world. Using data and technology has made trust visible and tangible, often in the form of beautiful, simple and convenient user interfaces. This has enabled people all around the world to scale their network of trusted relationships to unprecedented levels. For the first time in history, the social and relationship capital humanity has always relied on (aside from money as its formal equivalent) becomes visible and measurable. This gave birth to what I call *social capital markets* creating immense value for people. Relationship-driven business will likely redistribute value chains to make them fairer and more sustainable. The move towards transparency and responsible commerce in many ways coincides with global socio-economic digitisation and shifts in people's attitudes and interactions onto the digital economy infrastructure at our disposal.

Trust is what holds it all together. Facilitating trust building between strangers is perhaps the greatest achievement of this new digital world. Because trust offers a more wholesome concept of value creation than money (which is about value *distribution*). Its increasing dominance in our globalised socio-economic interactions will likely make for a kinder and happier collaboration – the ingenious lifeblood of our species. Fixing the inherent issues of the global economy today and moving forward, we must look at both social and economic capital in tandem, always. Trust naturally and conceptually incorporates both social and economic aspects of a relationship, which makes it such an interesting concept to begin with. Trust is, somewhat uniquely, concurrently associated with an increase in wealth and happiness. A healthy trusted relationship is always reciprocal and fair, intuitively, and naturally so. This means trust makes it much easier to identify and prevent inequality from manifesting. It generally tends to balance value exchanges, meaning the resulting win-win situation is as equitable as possible.

If the problem of the modern world is a focus on the means instead of the ends, does this mean that we will enjoy a better future by imagining a world in which more of our needs are met? This would take our eyes off the form factors with which we organise society and instead give us an opportunity to look at the desired outcomes. In many ways, yes. One of the most important aspects of designing the future, quite naturally, is to realign it to human need. If you've ever heard of human-centred design or customer centricity, this will appear logical. But a focus on what we don't have can all too easily derail into selfishness gospel. It's extremely hard to design for wants universally because we have a natural incentive to relate them to us and skew them in our favour. Part of it has to do

> One of the most important aspects of designing the future, quite naturally, is to realign it to human need.

with the fact that our current economic system is so extensively built on competition over collaboration that we assume this to be the default mode of interaction. This system focuses on selfish pursuit of resources and the promise that doing so will give us all we ever desire. It's a tempting idea to buy into.

This means we've outsourced the responsibility for attaining mutually beneficial outcomes to an abstract idea, thus seemingly legitimising our individual focus on self-serving interests. The biggest damage this thinking has done is convincing us that selfishness is the most pragmatic way for us to interact commercially. We built economic growth on this bedrock and those foundations have calcified over time. Paradoxically, the larger our cities and settlements grow that way, the lonelier we appear to become as individuals. It's highly questionable whether that really corroborates the idea that selfishness and the invisible hand create the *greater social good*. It is much more likely that the invisible hand has fed us a tempting but errant ideology; it then slapped us in the face over and over again with it. As the world faces a global surge in mental health issues, such as depression, with some branding it as a 'mental health epidemic', we may be wondering what is causing this – certainly not an oversupply of community and connection.

This is one of the many reasons I have been advocating for businesses, governments, and people to measure and enhance their value creation by measuring, managing, and designing for trust. Using some of what is happening in the digital *Trust Economy* as a role model to emulate and further evolve, this trust can become the shaping force in how we build our future economies and societies. In the digital economy, people easily trust by default. What makes this possible is a data layer giving us context about the people we are dealing with online, even if we don't know them in person. That allows us to build trusted relationships quickly, easily and at scale within the scaffoldings of digital tribes. By doing so, they allow us to do business more naturally and humanely, more in line with how we are wired to exist among others.

As you may recall from our earlier excursion into the matter, in prehistoric days, humanity used to live in tribal bands of up to a few hundred people, which relied on closely-knit collaboration, but stayed away from other tribes in general. They did not yet have the systems and tools available to interact with out-group members, like we so remarkably do on a global scale today. But, as we have also explored, along came an inflation of 'necessary distrust' and its associated inefficiencies and miseries. Uniquely, in such circumstances of distrust, humans may actually be more selfish in a group context than individually. In such conditions, intentions for collaborative win-win interaction are easily derailed into competitive win-lose transactions since incentives are dysfunctional and in favour of the latter. It risks corrupting economy and humanity.

> Digital trust intermediation made it possible for large communities consisting of millions of individuals to successfully self-govern and self-regulate for a specific purpose like finding a partner online.

Eventually, technological progress began to offer an alternative in the form of sharing economy models, which can be regarded as the pioneers of a new form of human socio-economic collaboration and interaction approach. Digital trust intermediation made it possible for large communities consisting of millions of individuals to successfully self-govern and self-regulate for a specific purpose like finding a partner online, selling second-hand goods on a virtual marketplace, or scouting for a gardener. Companies facilitating such platforms (or building them) are surfing the wave of this *new social capitalism* and are beginning to threaten many existing old economy businesses.

When we look at the progress introduced by widespread digitisation over the past decade, we can afford to be a little optimistic. The digital economy hasn't just connected us in unprecedented ways; it's also piloted new pathways for us to interact with people anywhere in the world. This approach isn't based on selfishness, but rather on sharing. It's facilitated by digital intermediaries connecting people to exchange value with each other. Many of these platforms that we've seen rise to fame in recent years have achieved substantial scale and distribution. Despite or perhaps because of this, they've managed to remain quintessentially social platforms. I cover the nature and value of these platforms in-depth in my first book, *The Trust Economy*, where I describe how many of the digital utilities we take for granted today connect us to others in such ways that we can trust strangers easily and without friction.

Technology and data play a huge role in this because they enable us to build relationships with strangers as if we knew these individuals and to magically do this effectively even at great scale. This is profound because we generally prefer to deal with people we trust when that option is available. Whilst money has removed some, or much, of the need to build trusting relationships in order to exchange value with each other, our nature still prefers situations in which we are able to deal on the basis of personal trust. Ask most people in business today and they will tell you trust matters substantially. The larger and more complex than the deal, the more that appears to be true. But strangely, we've built a systemic blueprint for the world in which relationships are treated as optional. The idea that money and governance are able to replace relationships as the foundation of human collaboration is intriguing, but fundamentally misguided. That's because, as we have seen, they promote competition and self-interest. Whenever we see such kind of behaviour, it creates tension. It's naturally going to be a zero-sum game.

If these individuals were instead inclined to collaborate, they might find a way of growing the pie – or at least dividing it fairly. All it requires is for everyone to play along, yet this is where distrust usually sabotages the effort. It's a prisoner's dilemma of sorts: Those courageous enough to trust put themselves at risk of being taken advantage off when others do not follow suit. Trust relies on reciprocity. Without it, others gain what we give up. This means that in a system built on distrust, we are all incentivised to keep it that way. In such a system, we have no choice but to be selfish and compete.

Today, we rely on governance and management approaches that cultivate this distrust in unprecedented ways. We mobilise an army of rules and regulation just to keep things together. The idea is that this distrust saves us from the anarchy that would result if we ever loosened our grip. With increasing global complexity and interaction between people from countless fields, backgrounds, and belief systems, we are feeling pressured into adding layers of additional distrust. These are making it increasingly difficult to do business, requiring us to jump through immense numbers of hoops just to prove ourselves a good business partner – a hilariously dysfunctional and vicious cycle of inefficiency. The idea that distrust by default is a safer option than trust is extremely dangerous, because it is an unfortunately compelling one in the modern world. Because humans are reciprocal by nature, this leads to distrust being met by ever-more distrust, right up until someone dares to break the cycle. It's not that we deliberately built our world on distrust; it's an adverse effect of how we chose to structure and administer our societies, as well as how we aim for productive collaboration on a global level.

The role of trust and business is becoming ever-more significant. Building systems based on distrust may effectively vet potential business partners, but it still doesn't fill the trust vacuum in an instant. For much of our business interactions, we still look for favourable context to establish some form of relationship with the other party and size them up before we decide how to proceed. In fact, the larger and more complex the deal, the more there is a need for us to understand the other. People know that trust-building to make it happen matters easily as much as the distrust-driven hoop-jumping that takes place. Both matter, but strikingly, the more trust there is, the less cumbersome the whole thing feels. Wouldn't it be wise, therefore, to build a system that recognises and respects that?

The digital *Trust Economy* has begun to reverse the interpersonal trust void experienced in many transactional markets. Thanks to the virtues of technology, trust can be scaled easily and cheaply, without losing much of its personal touch. To that effect, the digital economy has brought about a relationship renaissance in which the

> The digital economy has brought about a relationship renaissance in which the social connections we form with others, for personal and professional reasons, take centre stage.

social connections we form with others, for personal and professional reasons, take centre stage. You may doubt the value of social media, the sharing economy, or big tech overall, but it's hard to deny that the digital age opened up countless avenues for us to connect with each other and form relationships that are mutually beneficial and create value on the whole. Much of the digital disruption we are seeing across industries and countries may actually reinvent our socio-economic interactions. It means we are using digital to amplify our nature, rather than designing and force-fitting us into systems ignoring it, as we have inadvertently done in the past.

On the flipside, many global problems we face today show us other kind of progress we have achieved lacks sustainability and equity, leaving many needs unaddressed, and many questions unanswered – in the online and offline world alike. Perhaps our engine of progress is turning us into creatures we were never intended to be. If it didn't sound so sensationalist, I'd say we've created *one hell of a global economy.*

Endnotes

1   https://www.jstor.org/stable/1811581?seq=1
2   https://onlinelibrary.wiley.com/doi/abs/10.1111/1468-2427.00475

Chapter 6

THE SLOW DEATH OF INDUSTRIALISM

Why the next age won't be industrial

humane economy, fuelled by social capital and genuine mutual gain, is a promising scenario on our horizons. Humans are not industrial. If you think that's obvious, you are of course right. That raises the question why much of today's world is built on industrialist principles and how those principles have permeated beyond the mass manufacturing world into our lives and psyches. Combined with hyper-globalism as we have experienced for several decades now, industrialist principles have turned us into appendages or extensions of production and consumption more so than we perhaps appreciate. We are often unaware of how entrenched this thinking has become (ever wondered why your supervisor is called a 'line manager'?).

As Indian mystic Sadhguru observes so aptly, *"Human is not a resource"*.[1]

You don't have to be a mystic to realise that, but it helps to be somewhat more enlightened than your peers to recognise the detrimental nature of these semantics. Since human society is a smorgasbord of collective illusions which we use to coordinate our complex social economic behaviour, we ought to choose our metaphors wisely. Humans, by virtue of intellect, experience life in thought more than any other living thing. Again, stating the obvious, it means a change of the human condition for the better must start and end with our *world within*. Perception is pivotal to experience. The link between what happens to the outside world and what happens internally is our ability to sense. We sense the world around us differently, we will change not just within, but so will the human emissions that continue to shape this planet. The prevalent narrative seems to suggest that changes in the outside world are just about the outside world. Externalising the change, however, distances us from the process. It would be foolish to believe the magnificence and extent of human creation could've been achieved or would've been achieved independent of the collective mental programs we are running on.

> A change of the human condition for the better must start and end with our *world within*.

Humans are not industrial. They are intelligent and full of imagination. We need this imaginativeness to shift thinking and thereby doing away from a mental model which is so incompatible with human nature that it's causing much damage to people and planet all around. We must free ourselves from our default endorsement of everything capital and everything industrial, and transition to minimum viable capitalism and industrialism coupled with maximum viable humanism and trust.

This takes a systemic and collective rethink from within. Changes made solely to the outside world, however well-intentioned, can only ever amount to symptom relief. Real pervasive change will occur around us the moment something changes in our inner worlds. The legacy systems we have institutionalised to manage things in a certain way are a challenge to overcome, but that legacy is reinforced by its equivalent thinking. Once we change our internal algorithms, they will inevitably lead us to reimagine the external systems around us to accommodate something new and hopefully better.

Much of the dark side of the technological revolution, for instance, hails from the application of traditional economic thinking to the task of building a new digital economy. This is why we can see tech companies increasingly acting in the same potentially irresponsible ways as many other corporations. Most of the scandals that have rippled through the tech economy have amounted to grave, morally detrimental infringements on people's individual rights. This is interesting because it runs so contrary to the declarant purpose and mission of tech disruptors and it most certainly hasn't made the world a better place.

Countless examples could serve to illustrate this point, because it happens to be a universal one. I believe many businesses started with the true intention of bringing about positive change, but have fallen victim to the downsides of capitalism just like any corporation is at risk of doing today. Technology company's ability to amass a great amount of data and value – and with comparatively lesser effort than other organisations – is inherently dangerous. This is especially the case when such abilities merge with a culture of corporate greed and a compulsive need to put shareholders above everything else. The results can be truly devastating. When we look at some prominent incidents, we quickly realise that even the people who apparently stood to benefit from such deviant behaviour would eventually condone it. But why realise the problem only when the damage has already been done? How could dubious data harvesting, commercialisation, and exploitation ever seem to be a legitimate deed? For all its extraordinary achievements, human civilisation remains unrivalled in its penchant for hypocrisy. It's a divide we must examine, for many companies eventually brought down by their misconduct were hitherto role models and standard setters. And while we must appreciate equally their contributions to society and focus our efforts on enhancing those (as goes for all corporations), we must wonder why patterns of wrongdoing so persistently emerge.

While society likes to single out the culprits and shame them publicly for everyone else to bask in righteousness, this does nothing to address the actual issues at a systemic level. Employees in a toxic organisation can act truly cruel in a business setting *and* be perfectly nice people in their personal time. When we learn to understand and appreciate the human ability to exist effortlessly amidst obvious contradictions, we begin to realise how labels of 'good' and 'bad' miss the salient point – that we are a product of our environments, especially its human-made aspects.

All formal structures fall victim to ideology that created them. The reason we still operate on these premises and defend capitalism is because we have not yet reached global consensus on a better alternative to it. It is time, therefore, to pose the question of what socio-economic construct we should aim for next in order to be able to move forward and solve the issues that have cropped up globally. What will the future of organisation and collaboration look like?

Unlike any other human culture, the capitalist cult has been structurally reinforced in ways very few cultural traditions are anchored in our minds. Moving past this ideological debt requires us to acknowledge things that we implicitly know already but rarely verbalise. One of them is that the pursuit of material goods and capital corrupts us internally when it inspires us to attach great significance to our possessions and refrain from sharing them with others. It's actually quite ironic that we have been able to reward antisocial and personally devastating behaviour and brand it as a representation of success and individual wealth.

If we are to achieve and share global wealth and a sense of individual happiness, we already know what we are doing at present will not suffice to get us there. Industrialism has enabled the proliferation of thinking and doing squarely against human nature. It has been justified by the notion that this was the only option we had to progress as a species, before technological advancements pointed us to other possibilities. It's true that capitalism is a remarkable machine and extremely capable of organising people at scale, but so are the digital platforms we already use to do just that. So why don't we use what we have at our disposal today to build interaction models in which everyone is in charge and social and cultural customs and mutual agreements take precedence over central enforcement? Doing so would give us a system more compatible with human nature and leverage the ingenuity of culture and social dynamics in regulating human behaviour with mutuality and ease.

Because the industrial economy relies heavily on distrust-driven measures to regulate behaviour, it has stopped relying on people's common sense to ensure that what happens is acceptable. It's about the digital communities themselves. Powered by technology and data, we are already witnessing highly effective communities of shared trust in a common cause. Self-control but also peer regulation work in these environments. Harnessing this ability to empower people globally and rally them around shared causes could dramatically enhance the effectiveness of formally mandated control measures in place right now. Further, the more each and every one of us feels a shared responsibility, the better we can ease enforced restrictions we live with – such as pandemic-related ones. Doing so will evolve us from reactive to proactive behavioural conditioning in how we manage crises, catalyse change, and shape our future.

It's time that we understand that the *Trust Economy* offers so much more promise to humanity than a simple opportunity to sell second-hand goods, find accommodation, or hitch a ride. It's about trusting fellow humans and our collective value-add in shaping our future planet together. The current global outlook requires humanity to collaborate on a mega-scale to address the most significant challenges of our times. Such effective collaboration, as we have seen, is only possible with a foundation of trust. We now have a unique opportunity to bring humanity together and neutralise the adverse effects of industrialism, in the hopes that the effect will set a new precedent for global economic and social harmony.

Even if we look at the demand side of our economy, we can realise that industrialism will be less prolific across various aspects of our lives – at least the centralised hyper-scaled industrial production model finds itself confronted with better alternatives in certain areas, especially those where standardisation is no longer easily possible, demanded or desired. Nowadays, like everything else in our world, demand for goods and services has become much more complex. We are seeking ever greater customisation and personalised experiences based on the data and context that we share with those producing what we consume. This means supply chains have become more difficult on both ends and continue to do so. All this requires far more sophisticated understanding of value drivers across supply and value chains. It also incentivises us to simplify where we can, address gaps where value is leaking, and seize opportunities for creating value where it is latent.

In managing all of this ridiculous complexity, one-size-fits-all administrative approaches as we inherited from industrial thinking become extremely unsuitable. Of course, this is less true for producing the many essential goods and services humanity needs, which are still churned out by factories because this is the only way currently to meet the global need. But we will see a shift, even in core industrial manufacturing, towards more simplified, decentralised, and agile ways. One focus will be on maximising what we can make of the resources at our disposal, which are increasingly scarce. A core drawback of classic industrial manufacturing is that its demands for infrastructure can lead to clustering, so that certain areas end up having an oversupply of manufacturing capability. Output then must be distributed to all the areas where it is desired or required. In theory, this leads to beneficial specialisation and incentivises trade because everyone is encouraged to focus on a speciality and then trade with others. Trading and specialisation at a community level is usually very beneficial – but when it happens on a global level, it creates dependencies which often result in problematic power dynamics and even monopolistic behaviour. It happens because, unlike at a community level, mutual distrust between economic actors in a complex global system is high and mutual understanding correspondingly low. The shared universal trust in money is not enough to compensate for this. Friction and inequality are a natural result. In many ways, the global industrialist system has survived and thrived despite its downsides. That's perfectly understandable and fine, so long as we recognise its limits.

Endnote

1   https://www.ishaeducation.org/human-is-not-a-resource/

Chapter 7

INSTITUTION TO DISTRIBUTION
A wealth of empowerment

Transaction costs are a fact of life in the global economy. They are the price we pay for the connections that enable us to trade. As such, they're a central target area for digital solutions. Decentralisation and simplification, even of fundamental value chains, can address several challenges of transaction costs and possible inequalities. It may allow smaller, more remote, and less economically influential catchments to attain a similar standard of living as bigger urban areas by balancing their participation in global trade with greater self-sufficiency. We should take this as an opportunity for more equal and harmonious global trade and benefit from reasonable degrees of communal autonomy. As a result, we will likely realise many savings through reduced transport efforts, preserve local cultures and traditions through a preference for local and regional sourcing where possible, and eliminate quality and waste related issues in the process. Such a departure from purely industrialist thinking is likely to boost equality, reinvigorate disadvantaged areas, balance economic and social well-being, and ensure greater resourcefulness in the way we meet our needs and harvest required resources with sustainability in mind.

In food supply, we are already witnessing a nascent shift of the sort. In many countries, up to half of a supermarket's fresh produce is thrown away before having the chance to be consumed. Inefficiencies like these are spill-over effects of an industrial system which focuses on scaled production separated mostly from distribution to those requiring it. In such an environment supply and demand can create a rough equilibrium at least in theory – but in reality, there will be much waste. In a communal setting in which food is grown locally, regionally and based solely on the actual verifiable demand in the community, such waste ceases to be a problem. The same goes for other information asymmetries such as the origins and quality of produce on offer, as well as the unequal geographical distribution of value generated by the supply chain – in which those producing the raw materials often receive very little for their efforts.

In a system where local ownership provides what is required at the community level, demand and supply are in equilibrium and mutual trust ensures everyone makes a fair and reasonable living. Pathological dependencies on central and industrial production intermediaries and the associated pressures they exert are removed. The resultant system is likely to be fairer, generate far less waste and emissions, and may even be economically more viable and effective – because it's simpler, more local, and more humane. It is no surprise that the world's best foods are often still produced that way, but what works for luxury products, like delicatessen, should also be workable for the rest of the market.

It would be naïve to believe this could happen to replace much of the global goods movement we are used to. Likely, that won't happen anytime soon. What will happen, though, is that markets begin to respond to increased pressures for transparency across the supply chain, verifiable sustainability in manufacturing and trust in the fairness of the value proposition offered. Of course, many of the goods and services we consume today are created using sophisticated and expensive equipment and know-how only few possess. Technology is going to help us here, though. Massive technological innovation in recent years has actually brought space-age capabilities (such as computing power) from giant industrial complexes into people's homes and pockets. Given this is occurring at a remarkable pace, it is highly likely that we will be capable of more and more sophisticated and complex value creation activities independently of location and also increasingly independent of scale. It's no coincidence that we have seen a proliferation of home baking, brewing, curing, and fermenting in recent years (which has, ironically, also fuelled consumerism around these very same activities – but that is another debate). What it does mean, however, is that a garage in a small alpine village in Switzerland may 3D-print a car part for a local resident requiring a repair. The garage would pay a royalty to the manufacturer to download the design, 3D-print the part locally, and fit it for the customer. This saves on warehousing, transport, and administrative oversight on the one hand and is most likely going to be more beneficial for everyone involved: the cost of the part could be lower than previously – and still manufacturer and garage could make an equal or even more attractive gain from the parts and services supplied. Such distributed value creation enabled by technology will help us rebalance from an overtly industrial economy to a hybrid one, in which sensible localisation peacefully co-exists with global trade efficiencies and scale economies where it makes sense.

Soon enough, making one's own power or designing and manufacturing one's own health supplements could very much be the norm. Now add the increasing proliferation of remote working into the mix and it soon becomes evident that this model applies equally to product and service economy, with services easier still created in such a distributed fashion. Note how this balance of central coordination and decentralised creation actually simplifies matters significantly and offers many benefits to all those involved. Such hybrid approaches are likely here to stay. This possibility of moving past a default industrial dependency and its inevitable value and power concentration will profoundly impact our lives and possibly evolve the nature of business altogether. With more power resting more equally in the hands of the communities, we may well see the world become a more equitable place. Anyone who has experienced this first-hand will refuse any alternative version of the future. This means technology may not just be the answer to how we can evolve capitalism into a better and upgraded collaboration system. It is also likely to open up entirely new ways in which we create goods, services, and value for one another. This is more than eternal optimism; it is a very plausible direction based on what we are already seeing emerge today and a trend that has been massively accelerated by the recent pandemic experience.

However exciting our vision for the future of humanity, we will probably come to realise that many of the grand human achievements of centuries will continue to have some utility to our existence. As with everything, some things are worth being held onto and kept in certain quantities in which they continue to serve us. What we will want to ensure going forward though is that we refrain from adhering to yet another overly dominant ideology which could turn out destructive. Any form of black-and-white labelled thinking is extremely counter-productive to our grasp of reality. Doing so may appear like a delightful escape from living with uncertainty and drawing boundaries where there is no such thing as a clear line, but it distances us further from what's really going on.

We can certainly agree that no human system has ever succeeded in successfully making redundant human intellect. Sure, there are prophecies that artificial intelligence will finally lead us to that possibility, but I hope and wish that that never happens to you or me. Whenever I think about the future, it strikes me just how many bizarre predictions have been made about the human tomorrow and thereafter. Many of these predictions turn out hilariously inaccurate once the future actually arrives, because the way they were generated is often myopic and biased to begin with. Many times, we make predictions based on what we imagine might be true, rather than the facts presenting themselves. As anyone would intuitively know, the predictive power of tools rests to a significant extent on the faith of those using them. Trying to predict the next thing by observing external patterns is like observing tarot cards instead of the psychic and their client. If we really want to get a sneak peek into the future, we must take

> When we think differently, we act differently. This means humanity does have the power to rally around a worthwhile belief about a possible future and manifest it in the form of a self-fulfilling prophecy.

stock of the prevalent mindscape and target our change there. When we think differently, we act differently. This means humanity does have the power to rally around a worthwhile belief about a possible future and manifest it in the form of a self-fulfilling prophecy.

The next age won't be industrial because human nature isn't. You can turn anybody into a factory hand, but that doesn't turn them into a machine. You still have to live with their *humanness*, and so do they. If we're interested in the positive development of humanity overall, we must stop trying to industrialise human beings. We all need to see things for what they are, and this is especially true for people who believe industrialising people is a good idea.

Fortunately or unfortunately, *real* and useful change requires action on the part of those calling the shots. The easiest way to create progress is to demonstrate it. Once we can sense a new reality on the horizon, it becomes tangible enough to alter our minds. This is true for every innovative product or service and it's certainly true for every innovative idea that attained acceptance. As the saying goes, had you asked carriage owners in the late 1800s what they wanted, they'd have likely requested a faster horse. The future will be different from the present in fundamental ways, and that will change how humanity collaborates and lives on the whole. Whether people like it or not, the world is becoming more distributed in knowledge, power, and value. At least that's what is happening in much of the digital economy.

Overall, that's a pretty sweet thing, because – as aforementioned – it helps us reduce transaction costs. Transaction costs essentially accrue whenever we need to make an effort to move from a basis of low or no trust towards achieving a foundation upon which the transaction can be successfully based. This means that every time we interact with a stranger, our overall productivity is affected until bridges of trust are in place – which then benefit us through reducing transaction cost in future dealings. Fundamentally, creating transaction bridges for collaboration and trade is the lowest common objective of corporations and institutions we know today. All of these entities are trust intermediaries, connecting people to each other, as well as the resources, products, services, and anything else they may need. This naturally carries its own transaction cost. Brands are also built on a core of intermediation – in being a reliable choice and guarantee of sorts for us to get what we expect. We honour this service typically with a brand premium on top of the service or good procured.

Ironically, the efforts to overcome frictional inefficiency in trade have led to the creation of centralised and often powerful intermediaries. One can, therefore, say that corporate value creation is a by-product of the need for us to trade on a shared foundation of trust. The digital economy provides such a foundation at a far lesser cost and with significantly greater empowerment of the individuals involved. Companies that run these digital economy platforms and therefore own powerful digital trust intermediaries are among the most influential and profitable businesses we can currently find. But their corporate nature is more coincidence than necessity. As we have seen with several scaled peer-to-peer models, what social networks realise as corporations can be achieved at similar scale by volunteers alone and often free from commercial interests. The magnitude of projects like *Wikipedia* and *WordPress* is just the tip of the iceberg when it comes to the possibilities awaiting us in decades to come. This reinforces that we are increasingly able to transact, interact, and relate to each other at tremendous scale in highly productive ways without any corporate or other institutions needed in the process. This signals that we are entering an age of absolute empowerment in which every citizen can become enlightened and contribute to the well-being of the whole – and without the interference of systems which are too self-interested or inflexible to continuously serve the people they are designed to serve. Explaining the success of peer contributions through the idea of altruism alone may be too simple, however. When effective, contributors that invest time and effort in creating shared value know and trust this value will return to them. A productive society is built on initiative for the community. This eliminates many of the inefficiencies that more formalised approaches to social well-being require in order to do what they do. Perhaps, we can hope for a future in which collective well-being is yet again in the hands of communities looking after every member for the greater good. It would afford us many efficiency and effectiveness gains in the delivery of such support – at least in theory.

> This signals that we are entering an age of absolute empowerment in which every citizen can become enlightened and contribute to the well-being of the whole – and without the interference of systems which are too self-interested or inflexible to continuously serve the people they are designed to serve.

For example, many societies with well-established social welfare programmes administer such benefits through complicated systems. The same happens for charities collecting donations such that they can provide care to those in need. However well-intended this entire process may be, it can be horrendously inefficient and costly. Once you wrap your head around it, it's perfectly logical that direct initiative towards the greater good is the most effective way in which humans can create a healthy society of giving and taking. In order to even get close to this ideal scenario, there must first be a notion that everybody trusts in the idea that individual well-being results from shared well-being, rather than believing in magical welfare resulting purely from market forces and selfishness. We should find great comfort in the idea that contributing towards something shared is going to make us collectively and individually better off than stern self-interest. A famous Anne Frank quote goes, *"nobody has ever become poor by giving."*[1]

Overwhelming amounts of research, and frankly common sense, already suggest that human virtues focusing on our collective good make us individually happier and better off. It may well be that humanity took a few wrong turns since the advent of agriculture and that those wrong turns may have culminated in some detrimental thought patterns once industrialisation became the dominant way to be. While we cannot interview hunter-gatherers who dwelled Earth thousands of years ago about their individual well-being and contentedness with life, we can take a guess that they'd agree. More importantly, we can ameliorate human experience going forward by working towards a better global socio-economic status quo – and that's time well spent.

The digital age is offering us an opportunity for transformation towards a radically different humanity.

Old and new economy, each with its advantages and drawbacks, are distinct and coexisting realities we are a part of today. And they are increasingly merging into a new status quo. Many already blurred lines between the various contexts in which we exist will continue to blend and create a truly and genuinely different future in the process. However that manifests, we must ensure that it can inspire the best in people rather than bring out the worst. We must be careful to provide fertile ground for the right seeds to flourish and advance our species. What we empower now shall influence our fates like never before.

> We must be careful to provide fertile ground for the right seeds to flourish and advance our species. What we empower now shall influence our fates like never before.

Before we speak about the age of empowerment as an actual verity, we must recognise how we are empowered by the digital economy and hence why this term it is appropriate. The digital age presents a unique value proposition to humanity. It gives us an opportunity to reclaim a way of life and mode of economic interaction that suits our nature. Such a way of life is not purely transactional. In the digital world, transactions that we engage in nearly always also provide opportunity for a relationship layer to be established. Data describing both the transaction and the relationship help us understand the context of an individual or a deal we are evaluating. Trust plays a significant role in this meta-perspective, creating a relationship trail which there is the promise of future interactions and a corresponding reduction in transaction cost, at least in connection with the people involved. We find ourselves gravitating towards the same business partners, and of course the same social circles, over and over again – that tendency is fundamental enough to remain, but it may be increasingly counteracted by the ability to build trust easily and quickly with nearly anyone, anywhere. As we port our interactions into digital platforms, this will empower a great deal of new social and economic interactions.

You can think of online communities and even platforms equivalent of rotary clubs or other social organisations. In the real world, the shared bonds of trust we build in face-to-face interactions reside with us, even when the initial context (the club) is removed. In the virtual world, the initial and long-term links between trust bonds and the context they come to be in is a little stickier. This is because trust-building and value creation online is supported by a continuously growing data trail. Thanks to the largely standardised and low-cost provision of a digital environment in which people from all walks of life can build the necessary trust to interact, transact, and relate with each other, trust can be easily scaled. Fortunately, this means that the world is returning to more of a *Trust Economy* than an industrial one. Data and technology empower us to build trust with ease and empower trust intermediaries like those we use in our digital lives to champion high-trust environments in which transaction cost and individual frictions are kept to a minimum.

For the most part, the online social environments in which this occurs are far more accessible to all pockets of the global population than the offline country clubs where we find trusted business is done traditionally. Of course, it's hard to compare both worlds, but the metaphor here is that a greater number of people have access to others for the purpose of building bonds and trading value with each other. In real terms, this means that pretty much anybody in the world can become a digital entrepreneur and find their community and audience within the global digital ether. In the past, humans were tethered to their village, or at least to their sphere of society. The digital era gives us new opportunity to redefine and rediscover the circles we belong in and to build our presence in them. The many digital tribes coexisting today and the diverse sets of interests they lean towards represent a novel approach to organising significant aspects of our societies.

While communities in the digital world are dynamic and naturally agile, many of them are entirely informal and lack an offline equivalent structure that would formalise them and add administrative burden. Most digital forms of association succeed in building shared bonds of trust that don't require oversight or management by formal structures. Perhaps it is fair to say that this makes digital communities more entrepreneurial, meaning to say they tend to advance through initiative rather than merely progress based on protocol. Surely there are many good reasons to have societies and associations in the offline world, but those largely stem from a time where digital communities simply didn't exist.

Now the perhaps easiest way to start a movement is in a digital environment. The Internet is home to distributed social organisation. The distributed nature that empowers us as individuals is just as well a serious threat to central top-down social organisations in the form of public organs of economies, states, and international relations. The fact that the Internet is more or less regulated by the institutions it may well have the capacity to replace is an interesting detail – one that may limit the extent to which distributed global governance driven by data and technology will be allowed to occur. But before we are tempted to imagine a world run entirely by people and on the rails of the Internet, we must first understand the opportunities that digital empowerment lends to each and every one of us.

Endnote

1   *The Diary of Anne Frank*, 1952.

Chapter 8

DIGITAL BY DEFAULT
The interface revolution

M ost aspects of our everyday lives involve digital interfaces and corresponding customer experiences. Sandwiched between us and the rest of the world, they are our window to the world. This vantage point is often advantageous to those companies providing these interfaces to us, for they have access to the data and trust we place in their custody. Interfaces have always been valuable, even before the advent of digitisation. Owners of the interfaces between people are in a unique position to bridge the world in such a way that value flows reciprocally – and the smartest of interfaces know how to harvest this value. Harvesting value from any interface is of course a function of its ability to generate value to begin with. Interfaces are also always an intermediary; digital intermediaries have become very effective in connecting us with what we want and need. Their ability, like any interface, rests on their capacity to build trust and values so as to offer us a desirable mode for us to interact and transact with others. Traditionally, interfaces were, indeed, represented by actual faces, whilst nowadays we see a great deal of interfaces existing primarily or even purely in the digital world. Those trusted digital intermediaries have become very effective at connecting us for the exchange of value, sometimes even for high-value transactions – and doing so at a marginal cost to serve compared to that of actual people (i.e., human interfaces) who have made this their business. Other digital intermediaries prefer to augment human intermediaries, as is often the case in industries such as real estate or insurance.

Most important is that humanity tends to rely by default on intermediating bridges between us and other people, thereby leaving the job of generating trust between two unacquainted parties in the hand of an (assumed) neutral third. More so, in some ways every business makes a living off connecting different types of valuable inputs and transforming them into desirable products or services for consumption. A brand, in abstract terms, is also a symbolic bridge between someone seeking a certain proposition and the proposition on the market represented by the brand. In a perfect world, none of these things would technically be necessary. We would have perfect knowledge of all there is and such an ultimate ability to find the *best possible choice* every time. But because there is no such thing, we have come to rely on trust intermediaries of all shapes, sizes, and types – be they traditional brands, brokers, stock exchanges or their digital counterparts and equivalents. Every such intermediary is also automatically an interface. In most cases, all or at least part of the interface interacts with us digitally, to the extent that digital interfaces are now often the default mode of interaction in our socio-economic lives: we find directions on our maps app, choose holiday options through online booking sites, search for apartments on digital property platforms, and look for romantic partners on dating apps. We may find ourselves ordering a taxi from a ride hailing app even when there's one right in front of us – because many of us today go digital by default.

All these digital utilities should intend to make our lives easier by means of helping us find what we're looking for. Usually, this is done in exchange for a fee. Often, we will be influenced by the nature of the intermediary and its corresponding interface. This might occur by way of a conversation that we have with an insurance agent about suitable coverage options for ourselves, or in the form of an Internet search for a product that we intend to purchase online. In both scenarios, we're researching and preparing prospective transactions using an interface provided by a trust intermediary. In the former case, the intermediary is indeed a person; in the latter it is a digital proposition (the search engine). Both tend to represent a commercial entity whose principal business activity usually comprises intermediation of this sort.

Interfaces make use of miscellaneous historic and personal data in order to provide their services. For example, both the insurance agent and the search engine will make use of their experience and the inputs that I give them to serve me something of interest. They will aim to facilitate a transaction in which I find what I am looking for and they receive some sort of commercial value in return: commission, data about myself, or perhaps the opportunity to serve me again in the future – and possibly make a profit from this subsequent transaction. By helping me find what I am looking for, they theoretically create benefit for the party providing it, myself, and for themselves. Even supermarkets principally work this way, connecting shoppers with producers. Banks do exactly that for financial capital, agreeing to safekeep it for individuals and businesses while simultaneously lending it out to third parties in exchange for a percentage in interest charges. The most profitable businesses are in some way shape or form intermediation businesses, facilitating the trading activities that define our economic lives. But why would we choose to rely on all these intermediaries to help us trade, when we could simply procure everything directly from the source?

One explanation for this revolves around complexity, knowledge, and information asymmetries. Because the world is full of information and no individual knows all of it, information asymmetry creates a need, in turn, to consult an interface of sorts that will help us make sense of how we might achieve what we need and want to get done. This is especially relevant in a world dominated by complexity, including but not limited to language, cultural, administrative, and legal differences in contexts which may have an effect on what we intend to purchase. As the world becomes increasingly global, we interface with more and more different contexts and do so at an unprecedented pace, which means assistance in doing so is valuable. Even if it isn't something consumers would be willing to pay for, most businesses will gladly pay a commission to someone bringing them a customer. We typically refer to this as distribution, which is a key component of intermediary businesses. Whereas an online travel agent distributes various accommodation and transport services – building the bridge to prospective customers for these – a store selling appliances does the very same thing for household electronics. Increasingly, this happens in the digital realm because that is where many of us search for what we need and want by default. Digital interfaces serving us with consumption and/or connection opportunities have become dominant and there are a few important reasons for why this is so.

The first is their convenient availability at our disposal almost instantly through laptops or smartphones that we carry with us throughout the day. The mobilisation of the productivity technology that we rely on has made a significant influence on enabling such convenience to begin with. The second reason we turn to digital interfaces is a tempting value proposition, which often provide services to us free of charge or at a lower fee than interfaces with real faces. We must appreciate here that many digital interfaces are a sort of *precursor* to human interaction, promising to help us find the most suitable intermediary in the physical world on our behalf. This can sometimes even help us skip several traditional intermediaries in the value chain to connect directly with the people that have what we seek or are looking for what we can provide. Third is their versatility, helping us in an often broad array of areas. For example, price comparison engines on the Internet can cover almost anything from electronics to pet food or insurances and mortgages. Associated with each of those product and service categories are many types of primary interfaces, ranging from websites to retail stores to branches to agencies and so forth. If we researched each of those on our own time and initiative, we'd spend far more time procuring before we could start consuming. On the flipside, digital intermediaries tend to give us more options and choice, so the time they theoretically save us might be spent on evaluating a greater consideration set;

take for instance that a survey recently found that Europeans spend an average of 3.5 hours searching options for a single flight.[1]

> Technology can be the human-made equivalent of an all-seeing-eye, serving us a myriad of options for close to anything.

Technology can be the human-made equivalent of an all-seeing-eye, serving us a myriad of options for close to anything. Whether all that choice actually makes us better off is debatable, but we gladly take it anyway. Technology and the digital interfaces fronting them exert an ever-greater influence on our decisions and behaviour, almost equally in social and economic questions. Digital interfaces these days, by virtue of what they connect us to, shape whom we become friends with, whom we make babies with (or not), which jobs we are offered, where we choose to live, what products we buy, how we spend our free time and pretty much any other socio-economic decision. Relying on these for all our decision-making all the time means we tend to avail digital intermediaries excessively, without much conscious or qualifying thought. We do the same whenever we intend to be entertained. Every moment of boredom is treated with a glance at our screens in the hope of escaping our ennui by immersing in the temptations of the virtual world.

Because digital is very much part of our reality, its massive influence in our lives appears to hide in plain sight. What is posing as a helpful, seemingly neutral ally to our daily decision-making is actually after our data, time, and money. The fact that we are increasingly addicted to digital services is a highly convenient circumstance for those organisations providing them. When was the last time you consciously considered that your search results are *personalised to you*? When did it last occur to you that the things you buy and do might have been conditioned into you, with much of this conditioning happening online? Moreover *in vivo*, your social media feed may influence you as much as you influence it. In consequence, humans are merging with digital interfaces into cyborg creatures, occasionally walking into lamp posts while gazing at their phones and the many promises they harbour.

Assuming for a moment that our decisions might be largely mirror images of digital conditioning, it becomes increasingly difficult to differentiate what is real and what isn't. Purchase behaviour seems to suggest that many people take what is presented to them (especially on

> Assuming for a moment that our decisions might be largely mirror images of digital conditioning, it becomes increasingly difficult to differentiate what is real and what isn't.

digital interfaces) at face value: what you experience firsthand through a *digital façade* may become your impression of what's going on behind it. Recent generations who grew up with this in particular will easily equate interface quality with the quality of the product or service it represents. We have always known this as the packaging effect. Good packaging actually creates the illusion of elevated quality, which may or may not hold true. Attractive digital wrappers are exactly the same concept. If we take a liking to our bank relationship manager or real estate broker, we are much more likely to buy from them. Digital deception or influence is nothing new and probably not much different to its equivalent in the physical.

But unlike the tactile world, in which such influence takes a considerable amount of effort, it's fairly easy to manufacture with digital interfaces. On the Internet, a tree isn't necessarily a tree. Nothing is automatically what it seems. Since the Internet is an artificial world, smoke and mirrors may be any- and everything. Some of us even cultivate different digital identities compared to our real-world selves. In a way, the Internet is an echo chamber without a natural conscience, and phenomena like fake news and any other form of profitable deception thrive on it. The boundary between tangible and intangible is increasingly hard to draw, as is distinguishing between the surface and the substance underneath. One way to see it is that we are increasingly incentivised by the outside world to take things at face value, for speed, and convenience. Whenever we risk confusing the two, it complicates matters in the long run, leading us towards damaging shortcut judgements about the nature of things. This is something that we are already dealing with on a daily basis – for instance, when we painstakingly research our perfect hotel for a short getaway, only to realise it's nothing like reviews and photos online.

Interfaces and the Internet exhibit the same flaws as any human system of considerable magnitude. It is no question that they provide immense value to our everyday, but the opposite is also true, as for nearly everything human-made. Humanity has augmented earth's natural disasters with the potential for additional artificial disasters, such as tsunamis of influential misinformation proliferating on social media or quakes of cybercrime exposing the cracks in many security infrastructures. In our relentless creation of complex collaboration systems with good intention and great promise, we risk continuously and accidentally outsmarting ourselves. I find that both entertaining and endearing – but, most rationally, it is a huge systemic problem and the reason we are perpetually chasing our own tail, trying to innovate away the issues we have created through our impressive global progress.

> We are perpetually chasing our own tail, trying to innovate away the issues we have created through our impressive global progress.

Fake news, nationalism, populism, and protectionism are examples of how the unfortunate divergence between reality and perception is poisoning humankind. It's always been true that human behaviour is a function of what we *perceive* reality to be, rather than reality in itself. But in a less complex world, it was still possible to correct perspectives with ease and proceed to make informed decisions. Nowadays, the illusions facing us in every aspect of our lives, work and personal, make it exceptionally hard for us to form an independently objective opinion about the world. The quintessential irony of this information age is that the more information we have access to, the narrower many minds become.

The disconnect between what still exists of the old world and the advent of a new digital world has never been greater. This is a problem because all of us, like it or not, exist in both. Our modern struggle to align with this hybrid identity is a fact of life. As we connect our virtual and physical selves, the discrepancy between our thoughts, actions, and public persona and the many facets to our identity and expression become more varied than they already are. Most of us wear different hats in different social contexts, and our digitally equivalent existences have further added several hats to this already crowded coat rack of our social facets. We naturally exist somewhere within and between all this. The same goes for industries and businesses, some of which found themselves in a digital spotlight irrespective of whether or not they wanted it. Others successfully opted out of as much digital presence as possible; those existing in between these extremes had to find their place in all of it. Proactive and reactive forces at play here have a big impact on speed and scope at which this happens, but overall, digitisation has become the kind of party everybody feels obliged to attend, albeit with mixed enthusiasm.

> Digitisation has become the kind of party everybody feels obliged to attend, albeit with mixed enthusiasm.

But the offline world is far from dead. Many long-standing business relationships continue as they always have, some even by handshake. While digitisation promises to eliminate many frictions and transaction costs of doing business, existing high-trust business relationships already operate in a remarkably frictionless way, which means the marginal value-add of a digital equivalent way of doing business is comparatively smaller. I know people who have purchased cars from the same salesman over decades and will probably continue to do so because of the strong connection already prevalent. They might enjoy a digital augmentation of this relationship, but it doesn't carry as much significance. Most of the time, digital interfaces serve to make trust building and subsequent transacting easier and more effective, especially between parties who don't have such strong trusted bonds as yet. Once a commercial relationship unfolds, it tends to naturally acquire a personal relationship component *over time*. This is why digital interfaces should seek to augment human interaction, rather than seek to replace it entirely. All the same, digital trust intermediaries can make life much easier and faster for both sides. Commercial or social activity designed around single, non-repeating contact is inherently high risk because it tempts people to disregard the need for future trust building. Souvenir shops and tourist hotels or restaurants can fall into such a category; accordingly, their customer experience are typically forgettable. But even businesses targeting single-transaction markets should still focus on a longer horizon. After all, reputation and good old word-of-mouth is the best advertising that any business can afford. Human interfaces in the long-term can be more effective and less transactional than their digital equivalents, and every business should endeavour to cultivate both in harmony.

The vastness of the Internet means we are ever more spoilt for choice. With this, loyalty may not be an obvious choice. The interface revolution is incentivising faster and perhaps shorter decision horizons than we have been accustomed to making. Cultivating human touches, even simply through building digital interfaces capable of truly understanding customers and delivering an experience that makes them feel in good hands, can inspire loyalty via return business and advocacy. Often, whether something feels transactional is more important than whether the transaction is objectively efficient. Many of the best interfaces don't feel transactional at all. Streamlining transactional components naturally present in any business by using well-designed digital interfaces is highly advantageous (and increasingly expected). These make our lives easier by taking the burden off many exhaustive or cumbersome

> Cultivating human touches, even simply through building digital interfaces capable of truly understanding customers and delivering an experience that makes them feel in good hands, can inspire loyalty via return business and advocacy.

transactions that we previously needed to do offline as part of our regular socio-economic activities. However, we must also know how to draw the line between positive and excessive involvement of digital in our every breath and decision.

Rapid digitisation of information and communication has come with its own drawbacks, especially when carelessly applied. Compared to the old economy, this new economy evolves far more rapidly and is exceedingly more resourceful and capable of driving change. We can utilise this for better and for worse. In a way, the co-existence of the old and new world is a temporary dissonance which will resolve eventually. Digitisation of interfaces should both be a reflection and a contrast to how things used to be. Just like what preceded it, digital only works well when there is mutual trust. In its absence, digital interfaces may *appear* to make life easier, but they're often guilty of serving us endless legalese in the form of terms and conditions, simply making the process *feel* simpler and more convenient. The difference between signing a 30-page contract given to you by your insurance agent and clicking *'I have read and accept the terms and conditions'* is essentially that we consider the former grossly negligent and the latter a fact of everyday life. But both are equally problematic; we must be especially careful in situations where digital makes it more comfortable for us to behave irrationally. It's perfectly valid to argue that fine print is exasperating, but the solution is not to ever decrease the font size or hide it between a checkbox so that none of us read it. The solution is to bring that mountain of legalese down to the size of a speed bump, such that we

> The solution is to bring that mountain of legalese down to the size of a speed bump, such that we can deal with each other in mutual trust and confidence.

can deal with each other in mutual trust and confidence. Without thinking of the ways that we can use digital to fix the frictions of our commercial and social existences (rather than hide them), we risk avoiding the underlying problems that have brought about all this administrative friction – a belief that distrusting the people we interact and do business with is in some way beneficial to our own good, when it couldn't be further from the truth.

Equally, we would want to avoid digital anarchy in which there are no traditions, no terms and conditions, and no sense of what's ok and what isn't. Regulating technology has been tricky because of its fast and relentless evolution. Much as the digital (trust) economy is a world of possibilities, it's also a universe in which ignorance of beneficial social norms is a genuine threat. For instance, many people complaining online about a certain matter exercise little moderation because freedom of speech in a virtual world is enjoyed with at least partial anonymity. As Oscar Wilde put it, *"Man is least himself when he talks in his own person. Give him a mask, and he will tell you the truth."* But when that 'truth' disregards any and all social norms for airing it, much avoidable dissonance ensues. The same goes for standards of what should and shouldn't be commercialised and monetised online. Anyone able to use a smartphone or laptop these days can technically sell their 'content' to fans and followers on the Internet. Whatever the nature of such content, we can assume much of it would never see the light of day if the enterprising individuals disseminating it would sell via a booth in their local community. We must ensure that the digital

> We must ensure that the digital possibilities granted help us create a more frictionless world of digital interaction instead of a brave new world emphasising humanity's less delightful side.

possibilities granted help us create a more frictionless world of digital interaction instead of a brave new world emphasising humanity's less delightful side.

We must address overregulation in the old economy not by hiding it behind beautiful interfaces, but by fixing the root cause and preventing digitisation to grow over our heads even more than it already has. We must remember to treat it as an approach to solving problems, not a default for everything just because the possibility exists. We must also ensure that we preserve traditions and customs worth keeping since what's gone once is usually difficult to bring back. Accelerating progress is a fact of life, but productive only to the extent that we can tell apart what needs replacing from what's worth keeping. It's our duty to convince the youngest segment of the human population that values are not simply the moral manifestation of the shackles of the past. We must merge the conflicting nature of the offline and online world in such a way that we achieve inner and collective harmony. This calls for some much-needed introspection before we address that challenge.

Endnote

1 https://www.sabre.com/insights/releases/europeans-spend-longer-searching-for-flights-than-they-do-experiencing-them/

III

the future you

" We know hunger is temporary and still expect satiety to be permanent. "

Chapter 9

SIMPLICITY
Focusing on pure value

I t's possible there are things that you would like to change about your life. Perhaps this may revolve around spending more time on what matters, decluttering your environment, finding greater peace within your inner world or any other meaningful improvement you seek. Most likely, as you embark on your own journey towards getting there, you will realise that all of the above – and anything else you may pursue – simplifies your life. Personally, the joy of simplicity has always intrigued me. Take our appreciation for nature. It mostly rests on appreciation of the simplest of things – and some of those things have merely escaped our daily attention. I always wondered how something as existential as a night sky full of stars can leave us in so much awe. Take the human fascination for active volcanoes or the northern lights. Sure, the phenomena bringing about these realities are far from simple, yet the experience for us, as we bask in them, is. We are wired to enjoy the value of nature – as we are as much a part of it as *it* is a part of us – and I'm also convinced that we are wired to appreciate the joys of simplicity. Simplicity helps conserve energy otherwise wasted on decisions we could do without.

Much of our modern world seems to believe that the more choice in all aspects of life, the better. But we all intuitively know that too much or irrelevant choice is a nuisance. Consumer goods and services landscapes suffer from this considerably, creating choice and differentiation for the sake of it, typically, most industrially or mass-produced things are more similar than they are different. Truly, in today's commercial-scape, originality is rare. Seemingly abundant but insignificant choices create an illusion of differentiation in commoditised markets resembling, upon closer examination, a sea of sameness. The objective difference between competing laundry detergents or strategy consultancies often hardly reaches beyond brand formalities like packaging, façade, and corporate identity. Without additional context that would reveal a real difference, our best option is to go with personal preference or that mundane criterion of price. Whether we are in a supermarket or in enterprise procurement, we are taught to make the reasonable assumption that whatever differentiation we are pitched isn't always true to actual delivery.

> Seemingly abundant but insignificant choices create an illusion of differentiation in commoditised markets resembling, upon closer examination, a sea of sameness.

We know just as well that every detergent claiming to be the best choice is really just that – a choice – and that every consultancy claiming to have the most distinguished expertise simply just offers *an* expertise. On a global scale, we see countless versions of seemingly different same things. Some aspects of globalisation have transformed the bright spectrum of colour that is human diversity into the kind of greyish medley you get when you randomly mix different shades of paint. At a sector level, this is even more apparent. Pretty much every financial product is essentially the same, as are all petrol stations, cleaning services, and airports (with Changi Airport being the positive exception to the pattern, perhaps).

An interesting dilemma unfolds. Industrialisation principally favours standardisation and sameness. If you choose to set up a manufacturing site, you will likely set it up as is the common standard because that would be easiest, fastest, and cheapest. You would educate yourself about the way in which something you intend to make is typically produced, and perhaps hire people with experience doing so. In the end, you get your version or interpretation of a more or less standard product. It may carry your name, but to be original, you would need to innovate *key aspects* of your value creation. It could be the business model, manufacturing process, or customer experience (and ideally *should be* all of the above). But in the real world, convention deters you from doing anything originally. Thus, what you get is more commoditised products. Because originality and innovation can seem hard, we typically get more of the same. If in such a context you want to be different, you may resort to making your product more complicated, so that it is harder to copy. But that's not what your customers want – and you will likely still

> Because originality and innovation can seem hard, we typically get more of the same.

be copied anyway. Differentiation in those contexts is often synonymous for adding complexity few people want and nobody needs.

What it takes instead is entrepreneurial counter-intuition to challenge the pressures and noises of status quo bias. In a world as congested as it is, simplicity is a good way to address the originality challenge because it's such a rare commodity. Championing it successfully often transforms an entire industry, as the general market responds by doing what it does best – emulating. Simplicity thus becomes a problem solver, an answer for resolving complexity, and an approach to shifting the status quo towards something better. It's a potent driver of innovation.

But is simplicity really that simple? Not really. If you don't fully understand something, you won't be able to make it simple; at least, it won't be the right kind of simple. As Albert Einstein said, *"everything should be made as simple as possible, but not simpler."* So, there is a degree and type of simplicity that's a best alternative and solution to the pains of the cluttered, convoluted world we are often faced with. But simplicity is as much a destination as it is a mode of transport. When you look at simplicity from a *problem-solving* perspective, it becomes a much more dynamic concept. The world as we know it, and especially the world of business, is plagued

> When you look at simplicity from a *problem-solving* perspective, it becomes a much more dynamic concept.

with ever-expanding complexity as a by-product of many of the factors we examined. Even those among us who don't mind this complexity can hardly claim to see through it all, all of the time. This means that simplicity does offer itself as an elegant solution to make better sense of a world that's become a little bit too complex to grasp. Simplicity in action can, be hugely helpful and influential in making life easier. It's as much an outcome as a lens with which to perceive and change the world. Simplicity is, therefore, culture and philosophy, serving as a great asset for any organisation to have on its side.

Simplicity as a modus operandi and an outcome really transforms our experience and removes all which we find undesirable from view. A simple experience is delightful, especially when we don't expect it as the task at hand is generally a complex one. This is, naturally, where simplicity promises to generate the greatest commercial value. Simple experiences give us the satisfying feeling of fully grasping what's going on and reassures that we're in good hands. You could liken it to falling in love – everything is easy all of a sudden. It's a state of mind we crave and it's a profitable affair, particularly in an environment where complexity is pervasive and there's a lack of alternatives to it.

Come to think of it, even our personal social media content is simplicity in action. It's an interpretation and lens representing us instead of an *accurate* picture. Curation is an integral part of the process and simplifies the messaging to the audience, ideally such that it tells a congruent story worth paying attention to. Often, it works like a charm. We gravitate naturally towards simple things and stories. Combine both and you get a brand or business that is truly original and needs not compete in the same ways as others do – equally for personal as for organisational brands. Simplicity determines what we are more likely to pay attention to versus what drowns fatefully in (digital) high seas, swallowed by waves of communication and content. In the digital world, simplicity has almost become a *default expectation.*

More than ever, people expect the world to be simple. They expect to have simple solutions for even the biggest of challenges. But simplicity isn't merely about an interface making things *appear* simple, it's about *actually making them simple.* For example, when a child draws a rocket-ship and informs you that it will take off to space in a minute, it has just simplified space travel dramatically in its imagination. But that doesn't mean space travel has actually been advanced in any way. Building a better space craft that is simpler and perhaps cheaper and faster as a result takes far more effort than just making it seem so. Posting your favourite life moments on social does make you a storyteller, but it doesn't make your life any better. Great stories are simple, true – but the best stories in business are those that actually happen.

> When people think that complex problems need complex solutions, they forget that complexity is part of the reason the status quo even has problems to begin with.

Simplicity, then, should be viewed as the most effective lens with which to problem-solve. When people think that complex problems need complex solutions, they forget that complexity is part of the reason the status quo even has problems to begin with. Much is needlessly complicated; there is no surprise that this creates a vacuum of engagement waiting to be filled with something that's simply compelling. Nobody likes complexity, let alone engaging with it. As with people, in a sea of annoyance and sameness, only the originals truly stand out. Simplicity can be the answer, but in a universe of perpetually increasing entropy, it simply isn't the norm.

Most companies eventually fail by losing touch with the reason people do business with them to begin with. Complexity is a cause and also by-product of such lost focus. Conversely, an organisation effectively *focusing on the essence of its customers' needs* will gravitate towards operational simplicity because it will concentrate its resources on resolving customer pain points, thus making life simpler for them. It's the profitable thing to do. This approach is successful in keeping the company in business because it helps continuously provide relevant solutions to the market. Effective brands, for instance, help us simplify our decision on which product or service to purchase. We expect those very products and services to solve a variety of problems for us. Generally speaking, value propositions of *any and every kind* are effective to the extent that they're able to harvest value from solving a problem for their audiences. As you may have heard before, this way of thinking about value delivery is known as *jobs theory* (and no, this is not about Steve).

Jobs theory basically articulates that we 'hire' value propositions, such as products and services (including their respective interfaces), to do certain jobs for us. This implies that nothing we consume is a purpose, in itself, but instead fulfils a role for us. Without continuous feedback from users and other stakeholders, any industry risks losing touch with its audience. Having an effective feedback loop in place is the best strategy for any organisation to keep adjusting itself so as to deliver the kind of value appreciated by the

> Simplicity is the natural result of connecting people with the means to achieve a certain end in the best possible way.

people it serves. Simplicity is the natural result of connecting people with the means to achieve a certain end in the best possible way.

The intertwining of simplicity and consumption is a paradox since consuming more naturally adds to our lives. This doesn't happen purely because we are groomed into a cult of perpetual consumption, but because we see everything that we buy as an opportunity to achieve something for us. This, in turn, might make life, in general, simpler, and better for us. It doesn't always happen as a result, but it's the idea.

Ironically, the more gadgets or content that we use with the objective of enhancing our lives, the more complex it can become. A beautiful illustration of this phenomenon is the ever-growing stash of devices that require charging on a regular basis. Its original intent was the same as that of the washing machine when it entered households: to free up time and make life easier. We like to outsource complexity, usually in the form of hard work, to technology. And truly, over decades, this has given us considerably more free time. But do you think people living today *feel* that is the case? I'm under the impression that many people feel a sense of overload instead, which goes to show that the narrative of technology as the hero simplifying our lives isn't as simple as it initially seems. As many wise people know already, simplicity has more to do with solving a real problem elegantly than it does with deploying technology in search of an itch to scratch. Because simplicity takes more courage, focus, and dedication than jumping on the techno-centricity bandwagon or trotting behind the latest hype in classic sheep mentality, it's still a rarity across much of business.

Simplicity is the most powerful strategy for aligning people and giving a company focus, which it can mint into dramatically improved value delivery, ultimately leading to genuine differentiation. Companies with that advantage do not just lead in their sector; they also have a much easier time discovering new white space opportunities for applying their existing and perhaps latent skills, as well as resources, to new problem statements. The game changer with simplicity is witnessing how it transforms organisations. The relentless focus on solving problems that matter to the customer drives constant evolution. In this type of organisation, innovation is a natural part of everyday work and an organic driver of progress.

Simplicity bundles these efforts towards unilateral outcomes that serve the organisation's reason for being. The more significant the problems that a company solves and the simpler the solutions are to digest, the more value it will deliver on an ongoing basis. A clear purpose shared by everyone in the organisation gives this drive for simplicity a platform to be meaningful. And the reason why many companies end up with complexity is because they don't know *why they exist* to begin with. This is often coupled with an estrangement from their customers' problems in clear need of resolution. An organisation without purpose is like a fish without head: it might remain alive in the short term, but it's certainly not going places. Likewise, an organisation lacking simple direction is confused. In such work environments, the head doesn't know what the fins are doing and vice versa; the resulting forward motion is appropriately poor. Many of these coordination and interaction problems are eased by focus.

As you will have seen by now, focus and value creation naturally go hand in hand with simplicity. The *Pareto Principle* is a popular way of expressing this. It explains that 20% of something typically achieves 80% of the associated results. Some have even squared this *Pareto Principle*, arguing that, by the same logic, a whopping 64% of value must derive from only 4% of overall activities. Imagine almost two-thirds of your current value creation achieved with

4% of the inputs! More so, by redeploying 100% of your existing resources in a more focused manner, you could theoretically aim to achieve multiple times the current level of outputs with the same amount of inputs. A focused organisation is likely to be exponentially more effective. You shouldn't expect the *Pareto Principle* to offer any precise percentages, but the core principle tends to hold true – that most of our value creation emanates from a small portion of our activities. Focusing and simplifying naturally are great guideposts for making the most of what we have. This means that even a little bit of focus will go a long way for you.

For many tech companies, simplicity is already a desirable guiding principle. Brand names of many technology disruptors even reflect this desire to keep things simple: take companies like *Nest, Seed,* or *Medium.* All of these names suggest that the companies they represent are building something so simple, it can be expressed in an ordinary word symbolising the company's activities. I took a similar direction working on the *Circles(.life)* brand, now a household name in Singapore. The message was simply to connect people with their social circles – the real reason we do business with telecoms providers to begin with. Choosing a simple name and brand to represent your business and its job in customers' lives is a trend that's here to stay. But companies that go down this path do more than that. In the case of *Circles,* the mission revolves around fixing major trust gaps and dysfunctional practices in the status quo, such as telcos' habit of locking customers into long contracts. Companies that don't

> Companies that don't trust their customers (to remain with the company) will devise ingenious measures to protect their revenue and ruin the customer experience.

trust their customers (to remain with the company) will devise ingenious measures to protect their revenue and ruin the customer experience, such as subsidising phone purchases and contracts on a minimum duration of many months. If a company is willing to trust the customer and their own offering, they can offer cancellation at any time, knowing that the most valuable commercial relationships occur when the interests of all involved parties are aligned. By championing a so-termed 'no-commitment' post-paid plan, *Circles* gave customers the psychological safety of deciding for themselves whether they should stay or go. On top of that, the team recognised telco providers' obsession with selling minute-inundated plans had become an arms race completely ignorant of customers' emerging hunger for mobile data. Nowadays, we see that same arms race happening around gigabytes of data, demonstrating how immune many corporations are to learning from their past mistakes. By recognising a tectonic shift in the industry early on and uncovering a latent customer frustration with incumbent propositions, *Circles* turned into a success story that evolved the industry status quo. Companies that reinvent an industry by *simplifying existing propositions* are making a positive difference and forcing incumbents to adapt. Customer *empowerment* is often a natural spill-over effect associated with transformation towards simplification because simple things are much easier to understand and like. Keeping customers aware of what's going on is naturally easier when simplicity is a guiding principle, further leading us to the topic of transparency, which is of equal significance in this age of digital empowerment.

Chapter 10

DO YOU SEE WHAT I SEE?

Transparency above all

In a world with an ever-growing inventory of information, a plethora of knowledge and expertise is free these days *if you can find it*. But often finding what we need is somewhat of a challenge, and navigating it is a profitable business in itself. This is probably the reason why expert networks have shown double-digit growth in recent years; getting in touch with someone who already knows what you need to know saves a substantial amount of time and effort when information is abundant and of greatly varying quality. The same goes for consumer choices. For nearly any given service or product, there are a multitude of price points and form factors which are often hard to even compare with each other – let alone with their substitutes.

Challenges and opportunities in this world both seem greater than in the past, simply because the world has expanded for all of us. Transparency is, therefore, a key ingredient influencing our ability to navigate it. But how does transparency relate to trust? Doesn't it seem like trust would do away with the need for transparency altogether? Why would you need transparency if you trust someone? Look closer and the question is actually posed the wrong way. Instead, we must ask: why would we trust someone in the absence of transparency? We often do so without even realising it. Great brands and effective interfaces simplify things for us so that we can trust and decide quickly without having to work our way into the details. This is great, as long as these tell an honest and objective story of the organisation behind it. Willingness to embrace and display transparency is a great indicator that this is the case. Companies which have *nothing to hide* will be inclined to do so, knowing it validates the trust vested in them. This creates congruency between what things seem like and what they truly are. The same is true for people. Those individuals who are comfortable being themselves are naturally more trustworthy simply because they have the courage to be *authentic*. In recent times, authenticity and originality have experienced a massive comeback. A re-emerging emphasis on genuine, trusted relationships in global business symbolises a *'trust renaissance,'* inspired by the idea of a *'relationship renaissance'* described in *The Human Brand*.[1] Transparency makes the formation of healthy and equal trust-based relationships easier and more effective. Our relationship with companies and brands should be more than a transactional friends-with-benefits

> Companies which have *nothing to hide* will be inclined to do so, knowing it validates the trust vested in them. This creates congruency between what things seem like and what they truly are.

arrangements. It requires both sides to see deeper purpose in the interaction. Businesses looking out for customers' best interests will likely see this being met with loyal reciprocity.

What might seem daunting to put into action is actually straightforward because organisations are really just swarms of people fitted into structures of varying effectiveness – meaning they are really nothing but relationships. It does however require a chassis of people in an organisation to *behave like people* and solve problems without really getting in the way. Transparency is the required foundation for this to happen. It creates a safe space in which people can freely share what's going on – good and bad – for everyone's benefit.

The sense of psychological safety we tend to find in particularly high-performing teams is a product of mutual acceptance, alignment, and awareness. It becomes easy in such environments to find purpose and performance in any circumstance. As will be very evident once we dive into the topic of *purpose*, organisational behaviour exerts greatest influence of the whole on a company's future. It fascinates me how many companies seem completely oblivious to this. An example are corporate reactions to COVID-19. Exemplary organisations did what they could to take care of their employees and customers – and they will be positively remembered for their actions. But many other companies decided, instead, to proceed with sweeping layoffs *and* potentially accepted of government support all the same. There is no doubt to me that the former organisations have a brighter future ahead than the latter. Humans are a bit like elephants. We will remember who treated us well in times of crisis versus those who turned their back on us the moment things became tough. Organisational conscience isn't

> Organisational conscience isn't altruism; it's good business sense, especially on a long-term horizon.

altruism; it's good business sense, especially on a long-term horizon.

Like few events before it, this pandemic revealed striking behavioural patterns, especially in private and public sector approaches to dealing with it. Those who counted on transparency to maintain a mutual sense of trust and *collective supportive action* (rather than digging trenches of distrust through selective information sharing and excessive policing of people) have by now harvested the fruits of their approach. Meanwhile, the distrust camp has found itself increasingly powerless and at the mercy of forces beyond its control. Ironically, the *less you trust, the riskier that can be.* My explanation for this is expectation. Take insurance companies: the more they expect customers to cheat, the more safeguards they put in place to prevent it. Those measures make customers – especially the majority of honest ones – feel like they are being distrusted for no reason, prompting them to become annoyed and respond with distrust of their own, as well as a general dislike of the company. The less you like a company, the less you care about its financial position, and the more you fight for your own interests when dealing with it. This means customers of said insurance company will likely claim what they can and stand up for their customer rights, since they might assume the company only cares about itself. In such contexts, the mutual distrust poisons the interaction and potentially causes misery and loss for all parties involved.

This applies in the same way to personal relationships, such as for example marriages divided by distrust and fear of a cheating partner. Often, trust in such environments feels unattainable or unrealistic because both sides are worried that any gesture of goodwill might be abused. Transparent communication could alleviate this fear, but it will never happen unless there is a clear understanding that lack of trust is the root of the issue. Few of us are willingly transparent unless they expect the favour to be reciprocated over time, because permanent one-sided transparency can create a *power imbalance and vulnerability of one in the face of the other*. One-sided transparency is a threat we naturally avoid (when we can), just like we avoid taking a relaxing nap in an alligator's mouth.

Of course, everything changes once the said relationship of transparency and trust are in place. In that case, we are very well capable of tolerating even quite extreme vulnerability within this safe haven. We might indeed find it palatable to take a well-deserved rest in our befriended alligator's snout, knowing she would be as tragically opposed to the idea of having us for lunch as would we. This is the power of trust. For that power to become unleashed, transparency is often paramount. Transparency is a tool for us to form trusted bonds with those whose natural interests we perceive to differ from our own (such as dangerous reptiles or in-laws). Note the difference between the real and perceived danger is primarily a function of the presence or absence of trust. But, just like trust, transparency usually follows a gradual process in which gestures are reciprocally answered and mirrored in a form of a virtuous cycle. In its absence, the virtuous upward cycle turns into a vicious downward one. Transparency is a road to trust between various people and different interests. Lack thereof is a very slippery slope.

> Transparency offers us the opportunity to negotiate *common ground* through dialogue and open sharing. It's a path to discovering the potential opportunity in dancing with the diversity around us.

Transparency offers us the opportunity to negotiate *common ground* through dialogue and open sharing. It's a path to discovering the potential opportunity in dancing with the diversity around us. All of this helps us navigate each other's intentions. Better understanding others' intentions averts the many avoidable misunderstandings poisoning human interaction. It's a pledge to accept who we are and how we are different from others – and that this, in itself, is not a threat or reason for mutual distrust. With transparency, we can often avoid misunderstandings that are the root of evil in human interaction. Nobody in history started a war out of overboard empathy or understanding.

Misunderstandings, in particular, create the kind of friction that becomes far amplified in environments where *trust asymmetries or a lack of trust* exists. In the absence of trust, humans naturally form camps. As previously examined in this book, us–versus–them thinking becomes the logical and dangerous default. In such environments, we cannot help but *seek misunderstanding* because the divisions we have created through distrust makes us assume that others intend to take what's ours. This, of course, legitimises doing the same by others. In such situations, there are only zero-sum games, winners and losers, right and wrong. People are bound to misunderstand each other and, in fact, do so repeatedly. Taking a step back to contextualise this for all of humanity and we realise that, on a global scale, we often cannot resist the urge to misunderstand each other for the sake of preserving our fishbowl reality. This is where experiencing a shift towards *shared trust* can open our world to common ground hidden in plain sight and powerfully reconcile what we thought would never come together.

Working towards such mutual trust foundations makes intentions align and misunderstandings dissolve. Transparency helps us provide the context and data points to facilitate this in the best possible ways. Misunderstanding is already far less common in environments where trust has been allowed to become the default way that we meet others. Transparency greatly assists in cementing this fragile balance. In particular, it helps prevent information asymmetries that supply oxygen for the destructive flames of the self-serving. Information imbalances coerce people into following without awareness and give leaders the buoyancy to lead without conscience. Some organisations turn this opportunity for manipulation into strategies of deliberate misconduct, only made possible by withholding information and its concentration in the hands of a select few. Profit maximisation for an evil minority carried out on the backs of the majority is the result. Your inner cynic may identify this as shareholder maximisation's elevator pitch, but that shouldn't be so.

Every highly profitable and exploitative corporation usually faces an equally, if not more successful, ethically governed alternative among its peer group. This goes to show that we always have a choice, even if we are unaware of it. To become a hero in the playground of global markets, being a bully might not get you very far in the long run. If

> To become a hero in the playground of global markets, being a bully might not get you very far in the long run.

our economy of growth and scale automatically and inadvertedly turned us all into monsters, we should've given up hope in the future of humanity a long time ago. I'd rather assume the inherent goodness of human nature despite its evident flaws. And we should give more credit to those who lead by example. At the same time, we must do a better job of inhibiting those who exploit systems for their own (and only their own) gain. Imagine a world in which every economic entity is held accountable by its peers in the same way that we hold people in our social circles accountable for their conduct.

Transparency comes easy when we can believe others look out for our best interests; it coincidingly inspires us to do the same in return. For us, personal transparency can also give us more freedom. When we have data points that enable us to better understand our surroundings and remove some of the uncertainty of our environment, life usually becomes easier. Transparency is a mutual responsibility shared by us all, and what is true at corporate level is most certainly also true for us as individuals. Where the commercial world used to focus on preventing others to copy what they did, the emphasis is now shifting towards strategic partnerships and open collaboration. Similarly, we are seeing a return of barter-like agreements between individuals, much like you would borrow eggs from your neighbour if you were baking a cake and had run out of certain ingredients. That kind of neighbourhood camaraderie is perhaps less common in large metropolitan settlements these days, but it survives in many places. It creates a kind of social fibre that lives beyond the transaction in the form of social capital. As we have seen, many sharing economy platforms enable us to extend such neighbourhood communities to anyone. Proverbially, this means that the entire world can pretty much become our neighbour, and it's even possible for us to know more about those far away neighbours than the ones right next door.

As you can see, the data economy can be a gem enriching our lives tremendously when it is built around principles of mutual transparency and trust. No matter how innovative and trust enabling your product, you're still going to have to pay a law firm to create contractual legalese for you, which is based solely on the assumption that a wide variety of people and events could adversely affect you and require you to cover your backside so as to avoid significant damage. If anything illustrates our default tendency towards scepticism in distrust accurately, it is our modern legal conventions that we consider a necessity of being in business. But this also shows just how systemically businesses default to distrust in the commercial world and how much can still be changed for the better.

The core problem is that in a situation where both parties are following a convention of scepticism in distrust, any one party shifting towards trusting the other will be vulnerable to being taken advantage of. Distrust creates gridlock situations in which neither party is willing to share. Where

> Distrust creates gridlock situations in which neither party is willing to share. Where transparency is already a given, trust-based interaction may be possible over a handshake without incurring any of the work or cost of legal friction.

transparency is already a given, trust-based interaction may be possible over a handshake without incurring any of the work or cost of legal friction. But, in reality, there are few altruistic or truly balanced contracts, and the undercurrent of antagonism and conflict is always present to an extent. But many great examples of win-win agreements between different individuals and organisations do exist in practice. The default selfish orientation of legal routines in modern business creates a discrepancy between the relationship, content, and administration layers of commerce. In strong business relationships, contracts are but a formality – an important, but subordinate aspect of the deal.

The same applies to the relationship between us as customers and the organisations trying to serve us. Aligning interests here will help put an end to mutual exploitation. Selfishness motivates us to seek the best deal when we buy and when we sell. On a transactional level, the best deal for each party may not align in a shared goal, so that any negotiation is zero-sum by default, gaining or making concessions. This is a good opportunity to speak about its relationship with transparency. Mutual dissonance is unfortunately a common issue surrounding the usage of personal data with companies trying to harvest what they can get. This has prompted customers to become increasingly focused on minimising the data they share. What we should aim for instead is a situation in which we can trust companies to handle our data in *our* interest. In such an environment, companies can rely on us to furnish relevant data because we rely on them to treat it conscientiously and work with it in ways that benefit us and refrain from exploitation.

Data isn't the new oil; it's the new nuclear power and the heart of our digital economy. But it doesn't mean we must exploit people's data to succeed. The ethical approach is in fact dramatically more effective and, ultimately, more profitable too. Big tech CEOs nowadays generally talk privacy not only for altruistic reasons, but because it pays off. Whenever trust leaves, value always leaves with it. Think of the global Financial Crisis, that Diesel emissions scandal, and, of course, the global lockdown necessitated by COVID-19.

> Data isn't the new oil; it's the new nuclear power and the heart of our digital economy. But it doesn't mean we must exploit people's data to succeed. The ethical approach is in fact dramatically more effective and, ultimately, more profitable too.

It's hard to create new value, let alone sustainable progress, in the absence of trust. It means shared transparency and trust are paramount in the digital and data economy, as is the promise to turn exploitative win-lose dynamics into healthy win-win commercial relationships. How companies handle our data is a prime indicator of how much they understand the crucial importance of trust, especially in light of major data breaches.

When a company, industry, economy, or individual suffers a loss of trust, they are left worse off. This loss allows competitors to gain ground, making it easier for new entrants to establish and scale. It's just like in a petri-dish: the moment the nasty e-coli bacteria start decimating, other microorganisms hustle for their place. There's never been a better time to be the friendly probiotic bacteria. Since many successful tech companies resemble monopolies, we should seize opportunities sowed by giants' omissions, continuing the cycle of innovation into the next generation. It's going to make our world a little better for sure. One thing I've always particularly enjoyed about Silicon Valley is its role as a bubble of social capital, community, and transparency on a human-to-human level. Connections in the Valley are everything, just like every other part of the world – but there you are met with an open culture where you can simply get to know people. This type of culture facilitates meaningful exchanges of knowledge and resources to easily transpire. Part of this is the tendency to make do without NDAs. When this happens routinely, it indicates a high systemic assumption of the trustworthiness in others; that alone appears to work well enough to save everyone from excessive amounts of paperwork. But it's also a prudent step, since Silicon Valley, of all places, knows ideas are worth little without execution. Openly sharing what you plan on building incentivises everyone to actually go ahead and do it, knowing that in all probable cases someone else will attempt the same at some point.

> Openly sharing what you plan on building incentivises everyone to actually go ahead and do it, knowing that in all probable cases someone else will attempt the same at some point.

What's remarkable is that, in such an environment, we find collaboration quite naturally. Accordingly, competition is primarily focused on individuals trying to achieve their ambition – not necessarily against someone else, but mostly for their own sake. Our society and we as individuals prosper when we can have the privilege of working towards the goals that we believe in. Antagonism isn't necessary in such an environment where everyone is driven by the purpose of doing something great rather than by the desire to win over someone else. As many wise people have observed before, there is no lasting joy in personal gain at the deliberate expense of others. Even in sports, you'll notice that winning is treated as a personal accomplishment, and that when winner's behaviour veers towards triumphing over others, waves of aggression tend to follow. Such aggression is a given when everyone's focus is on taking from others and giving to themselves.

IP and patent law illustrates this systemic conflict quite practically. While concern around our work being stolen is valid, patents and intellectual property ownership may limit the ability of the right products, ideas, or methods to find their way into heads or hands. There is a very good reason why many people choose to transparently share their thinking and make their creations available to the world. It isn't called insanity; it's called content marketing – and it works because it starts by giving value to others, knowing full well that some of this value will return with interest. Ask any digital marketer about funnels and the necessity for quality content to pique curiosity and manifest outcomes. I'm sure they will talk about similar things, and if they're ahead of the game, they'll also talk about the importance of building trust.

In the data economy, this is more evident than ever. The more your customers trust you, the more willing they are to share their data with you. Data quality and quantity makes your product more valuable, which leads customers to trust you even more. It's a virtuous cycle. The more you have trust on your side, the more likely people will see you as unique. I like to think that trust creates mental monopolies. When you trust something is the best or only option, it's hard for anything else to compete. With the virtue of transparency, we can see one world through all of our countless perspectives and reconnect what was subjected to division before us. It's our chance to meet eye-to-eye instead of eye-for-an-eye.

Do you see what I see? Do you hear the whispers of the future and feel the winds of change?

Endnote

1 https://www.amazon.com/Human-Brand-Relate-Products-Companies-ebook/dp/B00EFB44ES

Chapter 11

NEED FOR NEEDS

Enabling the right choices with design
thinking beyond propositions and users

There's a saying that when the heavens want to punish us, they give us what we want. As you may have begun to imagine, organisations and societies of the future are well advised to focus their energies on meeting shared human needs over supporting a selfish expression of individual wants. Needs unite humanity, whereas wants convince us that such unity is illusionary. Disagree as you may, I have yet to meet a sizeable number of people who attained happiness by pursuing their every want; but I personally have experienced the liberation of reflecting on the often simple human needs that make us human. In *Design for the Real World*, Victor Papanek diagnoses the modern world (at the time of writing, this meant 1970s America) with an unhealthy obsession for concentrating industrial-economic resources on making the superfluous look pretty. Designing for the 1% as opposed to solving real-world problems and extending the benefits of solutions to the remaining 99% was already an issue a half century ago. Technology innovation has made many everyday luxuries (such as air travel) dramatically more affordable since, but the observations still hold in principle.

> Much of design follows the money, paradoxically concentrating its resources on making unnecessary things compelling as opposed to solving problems whose resolution would truly and sustainably improve the human condition.

Much of design follows the money, paradoxically concentrating its resources on making unnecessary things compelling as opposed to solving problems whose resolution would truly and sustainably improve the human condition. Some of the pressing global issues Papanek identified back then sound all too familiar: increasing incidence of abnormal human behaviour caused by rapid urbanisation, over-reliance on single-pilot automobiles with high fuel consumption-congesting cities, excessive globalisation and environmental destruction, and ineffectively slow progress on policy reformation and systemic innovation, plus a vacuum of purpose in corporate employees.

Papanek proposed a refocus on designing human environments for interaction over anonymity, making the shift towards vehicle electrification and sharing systems, championing regional and local value chains, concentrating more first-world attention on solving global issues, and giving corporate warriors meaning by mandating them to solve problems for the public good. This might translate into catering to people with disabilities or creating consciously, so as to avert the side-effects of consumption. Inclusive, sustainable design based on universal need seems to be the direction here. While optimism would make me believe otherwise, it appears as though we have enjoyed little success in addressing these systemic issues over the past half-century. Rather, we find ourselves facing larger, more urgent versions of these very same issues right here in our third decade of the 21st century. This indicates that the scale of the problems at-hand have increased faster than our ability and willingness to solve them. In Papanek's 1970s explanation for this, he observes that:

"Greatly accelerated technological change has been used to create technological obsolescence. This year's product often incorporates enough technical changes to make it really superior to last year's offering. The economy of the marketplace, however, is still geared to a static philosophy of 'purchasing-owning' rather than a dynamic one of 'leasing-using', and price policy has not resulted in lowered consumer cost. If a television set, for instance, is to be an every-year affair, rather than a once-in-a-lifetime purchase, the price must reflect it. Instead, the real values of real things have been driven out by false values of false things, a sort of Gresham's Law of Design."[1]

Sounds like your latest smartphone purchase? People increasingly live in an artificial and senseless world with little meaning. A lot of it boils down to misalignment and dissonance between people driven to misunderstand each other. How could we have ended up here? A bold hypothesis to consider is humanity's tendency to ignore its real *needs* in favour of artificial *wants*. This is a major part of the philosophy churning the cogs of our global economic system.

Before we get to it, I'm not someone to criticise the default globalisation defining 21st century living. I do believe that our immense possibilities and choices in this world are definitely a great thing worth keeping, provided we make use of them in ways that serve others and ourselves. Borrowing that infamous movie line, "*With great power comes great responsibility.*"[2] How we make use of the immense universe of possibility at our fingertips is a main variable determining whether all this power will sabotage us or make us into the most wholesome version of humanity ever to exist. My main focus is on analysing the side-effects and what they tell us about the *real story* versus our initial intentions behind the systems and societies we built. I think it's a remarkable achievement that the world is as peaceful as it is, and that our way of life can offer so much beauty and functionality despite the fact that it's inherently troubled.

I'm equally glad to see many global organisations treat transformation as a new normal, fundamentally questioning the way they create value and open up to new approaches. Over the past decade, I've seen a constant rise in global interest towards design thinking, digital transformation, corporate innovation, customer experience, trend foresight, lean start-up models, business design, agility, the future of work, open-sourcing, and peer-to-peer marketplaces, as well as *Trust Economy* philosophies and methodologies. Having spanned my corporate, start-up and advisory career path across those fields, and especially at the interfaces where these fields interconnect, I have reason for continued optimism.

I'm passionately *for* a new type of globalism in which we make use of all this interest and intention toward a more sustainable world. I believe in combining all the wonderful possibilities of globalisation with a dedicated focus on lasting positive impact. Often, all it takes is a change in perspective, and I've always found thinking outside the box refreshing. Over the years, I took some of my observations back into the box to build a bridge between *the world that is* and *the world that could be*. Much of it entails switching our attention from what we want (which is usually highly fragmented and shaped by the status quo) towards what we need (which is almost always simple, timeless, universal, and substantially more fulfilling than catering to yet another one of our wants).

Shifting to a new reality may sound daunting, but take some of our most famous fictional stories, such as *Harry Potter* or *Star Wars*. They've described in large detail an *alternate reality*, much like the way video games immerse us in a different world with different roles and a different kind of society. Much of the detailing surrounding such alternate realities feels relatively realistic; whenever immersed in these worlds, they temporarily become our world, too. The difference between such worlds and the world we refer to as the 'real' reality is that the real world is operationally reinforced in everyday life. Pretty much everything humanity rests on these days to govern itself and organise human life is artificial and somewhat illusory, but we very rarely seem aware of that fact. Before governments and their various organs became real, they existed first in our shared imagination.

If they were to cease existing in that imagination, they would also cease to exist in reality – at least if we all built a collective consensus around them no longer existing. This illustrates just how blurred the lines between natural and artificial really are. Those lines are, of course, increasingly blurred with the advent of digital reality.

What this tells us is that many children's books were right: we can (pretend to) be anything we want to be (but it only works if we do it collectively). Imagining is the first step, and this requires us to take stock of what works well right now and what doesn't, so that we can imagine a better artificial system and make it real. If we choose to keep focusing on personal wants at the expense of shared needs, whatever is in place right now may seem adequate enough. Many people want life to remain the same, feel like they and society have made the right choices, and focus on what is already on their horizon. But our world would serve us better if it revolved around what we needed more than what we wanted, in the same way that having oat bran for breakfast every morning serves us better than a croissant. Unfortunately, the oat bran is the harder sell, which explains why our commercial world tends to be built around shallow wants more so than deeper needs.

> Having oat bran for breakfast every morning serves us better than a croissant. Unfortunately, the oat bran is the harder sell, which explains why our commercial world tends to be built around shallow wants more so than deeper needs.

Focusing on *needs,* logically, allows us to understand what's right for us and for the world, and evaluate at sensible distance whether the human creations defining our lives today serve our best interests. Many of the world's innovative and valuable companies already assume such a pure problem-solving mindset to uncover deep-rooted needs (and corresponding surface-level behaviours) to transform them into universally successful value propositions in the form of products, services, and ideas. Their skill is unearthing important needs and combining them with important wants – similar to serving your dog medicine hidden inside a delicious treat.

If the problem of the modern world is a focus on the means instead of the ends, does this imply that we will enjoy a better future by focusing on the needs instead? In many ways, yes. This would take our eyes off the form factors with which we organise society – and instead give us an opportunity to look at the desired outcomes. One of the most important aspects of designing the future, quite naturally, is to realign it to human need. If you've ever heard of human-centred design or customer centricity, this will appear logical.

By making an effort to explore this human depth, we can appreciate that universal shared human needs unite us. While they often manifest on the surface as a number of far less meaningful wants, addressing deeper needs cuts through the clutter of most consumer research, which seems preoccupied with *surface level analysis of what people want*, or worse: what they *say they want*. It may be this unfortunate preoccupation with superficiality that leads a majority of new products to fail, irrespective of the amount of research that goes into them. Uncovering deeper, less visible needs and prioritising them over catering to far less meaningful wants pays off. Coupled with actual user inputs and feedback, it can culminate in extraordinary products with enviable market success for the companies that do so. Those companies also coincidentally own many of the brands and voices people actually listen to. While a vast majority of organisations must shout to be heard, a privileged few need not raise their voice to receive all the attention. Such exceptions to the rule are great at understanding us much deeper than the rest,

> Addressing deeper needs cuts through the clutter of most consumer research, which seems preoccupied with *surface level analysis of what people want*, or worse: what they *say they want*.

maybe even deeper than we understand ourselves. Perhaps asking people what they want is futile; giving them what they *need* in a packaging they *want* is much, much better.

Indeed, knowing people's latent underlying needs by investing in their discovery and excavation leads to dramatically greater outcomes and makes for mutual gain: we knowingly and willingly pay more for things that we deeply resonate with. Needs-driven companies are very good at outperforming their competition; in fact, they rarely have to compete to begin with because they understand what nobody else seems to see or appreciate. Their ability to get to the source of what drives us instead of being distracted by the diversions of our various wants and opinions gives them a far better understanding of what to do and where to focus.

> Needs-driven companies are very good at outperforming their competition; in fact, they rarely have to compete to begin with because they understand what nobody else seems to see or appreciate.

Organisations and people operating that way also often apply this to the way they interface with people. For instance, organisations that recognise peoples' need for belonging and care naturally treat customers and employees differently and with more empathy. Companies focusing on needs know that money, beyond hygiene levels, *isn't* a universal human need while community, social identity, and trust are. Anybody thinking this way will understand that care and excellent service might be more valuable to a customer than offering the cheapest price.

Those players aren't competing *with* their industry or market *for* customers, but they are collaborating *with* their stakeholders to compete with less optimal value propositions. Their competition is channelled into an ethical and purposeful pursuit, rather than wanting to win for the sake of individual enrichment or pleasure. And, come to think of it, we should all eradicate toxic legacies and replace them with what invigorates us. Companies focusing on customer collaboration are better off by choice than those looking jealously over the fence to catch and copy anything their competitors are doing – irrespective of whether or not it generates any tangible customer value. A (re-)focus on shared human needs is really going to be key to better utilise what we built and evolved over centuries, especially over our last decades of rapid technological and digital ascent. As it so happens, this is also the recipe for individual happiness and well-being at large.

Happiness and well-being, just like focusing on needs, has to do with embracing constraints. This will be a red thread for the next chapter on living our best lives. Paradoxical as it may seem at first, constraints are vital to our happiness. They invigorate our imagination, creativity, and ability to pour all of that into something satisfying for our lives. Lack of self-restraint leaves us dissatisfied because we can only ever meet a portion of our insatiable appetite for wanting. It's a great recipe for self-inflicted misery, at least when we worship wants as if they represented what was really best for us.

Endnotes

1   https://designopendata.files.wordpress.com/2014/05/design-for-the-real-world-victor-papanek.pdf

2   This proverb is popularised by Spider-Man.

Chapter 12

THE KALE DOUGHNUT
Inspiring us to live our best lives

Asking for the right things and making good decisions truly is the origin of a great life. Our best life is something which may seem like a challenge to obtain, but it shouldn't feel like an unsurmountable one. Much of the disconnect between who we are and who we *could or should be* is created by a want-focused society rendering itself in a perpetual state of deprivation. There is a natural limit to what we truly need, but there is no such limit to wants. But before you misread the practice of listening to your own needs as a form of restraint, it's time to appreciate just how important constraints are to a life well-lived. My favourite way of illustrating this is by way of your personal dreams – say your dream future house.

Imagine you had unlimited options and funds for building your dream house. If you're an exceptionally focused and disciplined person, you'd perhaps be able to tell me promptly and exactly what you'd build. If you're like most people, though, you'd explore countless alternatives in an ever-expanding universe of possibilities. Then, when asked to settle for your final choice, you might try to do what you can to perfect your plan. But, by the time it's put into action, there's a chance you won't feel wholesome about it. What about all the other options that you may have considered or those options you missed out on to begin with? My guess is that ultimately, you wouldn't be all that happy with your dream house in spite of it *seeming* like a great opportunity to build anything you like. The problem with doing anything in the absence of real-world constraints is that you have too many options to choose from. You regret at least part of the choices you end up making.

This is what can happen when you translate the abstract into concrete without a very clear direction in mind, constraints to think about, challenges to resolve, and contextual dependencies to consider. It's akin to being a kid in a candy store, blinded by the sweets on display but leaving with a yearning for more (and cavities waiting to happen). In other words, a lack of constraints *isn't* going to fuel your creativity; it's going to jam your gearbox in perpetual pondering about what *could be*. Vague dreams exist completely independent of reality and accordingly can never represent what would truly serve us. This is before we even assess an individual's ability to actually imagine and express what it is they're actually seeking.

It's very easy to sense check that, especially when it comes to our simple daily wants, such as sleeping in, skipping exercise, decimating doughnuts, complaining about something or other, and arguing with people about nothing in particular. Only if we tie these behaviours back to some kind of overarching purpose can they make any sense *at all*. If instead we did what we know we should be doing, such as being kind and compassionate, flossing, eating that delicious kale salad, taking time to learn something new every day, treating our body to the healthy movement it needs, or leaving our smartphone alone for the day, we know we'd feel better at the end of the day. So why don't we do that instead?

Our world has become so intoxicated with a culture of *wanting* that it made us want to forget many of the age-old virtues of a life well-lived. For this, as always, we see the beauty of a different philosophy. I think it's fair to say that everybody on some level would like to live their best life, and that not many of us have truly succeeded in this pursuit. That's perfectly fine because we and the world around us are all a work in progress – and with that, ever-evolving. Hopefully, that evolution will be for the greater good, instead of our demise.

But temptation often gets the best of us, especially in an oversaturated world of constant stimulation in which we are bombarded not just with our own wants, but with countless suggestions for all the things we *should want, right now*. Yet the promise of a happy life as a direct result of these temptations is totally illusory. Happiness isn't a by-product of consumerism. Consumerism is a form of mental junk food promising us happiness on sale. It's a refreshing drink of saltwater in the desert that will keep us forever hooked. Happiness is a state of mind with which we live life. That state relies not on consumption to become real, but on a choice to live life independent of the false promises saturating our attention and senses. It is enough to observe honeymooners on a remote island resort spending hours taking selfies to understand that many of us are caught in a world of compulsion, distracting ourselves from any genuine life experience in the present moment. It's probably going to drive humanity insane, if that hasn't already happened.

> Many of us are caught in a world of compulsion, distracting ourselves from any genuine life experience in the present moment.

But let's start with yourself. When was the last time you devoted your full attention to chirping birds, fragrant flowers on the roadside, or the joy of a friend's presence? When did you last feel genuinely at peace with yourself and the world? As our private and professional lives are harder to separate thanks to an omni-connected workplace and our looming digital existence, we constantly swivel our attention in between – browsing Instagram at our desks, checking work mail on a Sunday, and so on. I've noticed this ongoing alternation between the roles and value systems in which we operate makes life more stressful and numbs the senses. It's like trying on dozens of colognes in a drugstore; after sampling a few, all blend into a sea of sameness. Variety may be the spice of life, but too much of it leads us to check out. It's especially apparent in the lightning-fast shift between work and play. We are constantly on-off-on-off, attempting to live to the fullest while simultaneously recovering from countless stimuli inundating our synapses.

Remember your last vacation? Arrive in hotel, impatiently ask for wi-fi code, check your email, decide to respond sometime later, take a photo of the hotel lobby, vaguely listen to the receptionist's welcome, follow them to your room while selecting appropriate hashtags, almost run into another person in the elevator, nearly freak out because wi-fi connection drops during the elevator ride, arrive in room, browse through a social feed, jealously note your friend's long weekend in the Maldives, check out the resort's website, almost forget that you're here to relax with your girlfriend who has been trying to strike up a conversation with you for the past half-hour, realise you forgot to draw local currency, check your maps app for recommended restaurants in your area, read reviews of your own hotel, miss most of the picturesque sunset (but at least capture the rest on HD video), take a selfie, respond to a few emails on your phone, accidentally confuse your parents with a vulgarity composed by your smartphone's autocorrect, browse your dozen chat groups, ignore a bunch of messages because you don't know what to say, discover a promotion at your hotel restaurant, spend half an hour snapping pictures of your food, eat your lukewarm mains while updating your social profile...

Exaggerated perhaps, but strikingly close to reality. This constant on and off is dysfunctional. Inundation with stimuli overexcites our neurons. In a nutshell, we resemble a broken light switch and, just like a light bulb doesn't handle this for long, neither do we.

In response, we shut ourselves off from life. Multitasking becomes an accidental narcotic. Rather than resolving the struggle between our indecisiveness and the need for focus and rest in a world awash with options, we simply tone down our involvement in life. This, of course, is in an attempt to recover from the firework of stimuli without needing to trade off on variety and the perceived excitement of abundant choices. As our *FOMO* driven selves attempt to pursue the most from life, we paradoxically end up with much less. Take all-you-can-eat buffets. Why would we prefer to binge on unlimited supply of a countless mediocre dishes, as opposed to spending wisely on a few great ones? Whenever we substitute choice for quality (of life), we are only fooling ourselves.

> The more we attempt to escape monotony, the more it conquers our lives. Monotony is a response of the mind, not a product of the world we live in.

In other words, the more we attempt to escape monotony, the more it conquers our lives. Monotony is a response of the mind, not a product of the world we live in. We ought to allow our brains to recover and re-attune them to the simple beauty of existence. It can manifest as the fascination that naturally exists within every one of us if we put our mind to it. It's a powerful enabler of gratitude and the ability to enjoy life's small pleasures, but also its great blessings.

Focus is the opposite of monotony. We need great focus to capture the moment, which is all that is ever given to us. You'll only ever live in the present. Unless you build capacity for presence in the here and now, there'll be little joy to look back on or forward to. Once we make the conscious trade-off to be fully present and in charge, the good and bad things life throws our way have purpose. Focus makes us resilient towards setbacks and helps us turn them into opportunities for growth and advancement. Escaping real life hardly ever leads to great ideas. Instead, it leads to emptiness. Optimistic realism and self-discipline are the better way; we must build an economy around enabling us to get there, instead of keeping us at bay from finding peace that way.

Some of us struggle with choices because they seem to imply responsibility for potential consequences. Accepting known trade-offs and opportunity cost appears more painful at times than unknown (and less predictable) risk. If you are a little bit of everything or have achieved a little bit in various fields, I'd say you've probably incurred monumental opportunity cost. It's like attempting to hammer a flat piece of metal into the wall. There's a reason nails are pointy. We only have so much force to apply and spreading it thin diminishes our ability to impact. Even if your energy exceeds everyone else's, you're better off hammering one at a time. The enemy of focus is dilution.

What does it all mean? Dismiss the idea of fast alternation between 'on' and 'off' states. Dedicate your attention to one thing at a time and give it your 100%. Move from deep flow (full presence in whatever you are doing) to completely letting go (bringing back attention to yourself and resting your mind). Avoid succumbing to the countless stimuli prompting you to compulsively check your email or restlessly alternate between a little work and a little play. As soon as you consciously move from deep work to deep play, your life automatically slows down, and you'll have more time for enjoying. You'll make progress like never before and live intensely again. Start today. Go birdwatching in the park, do that thing you've been wanting to do for so long, or just reflect. You're onto something really great.

It seems relatively simple, in theory. Why do so many people say behaviour change is tough? For example, reviews of wellness apps concluded few were maximally effective in changing behaviour.[1] Why? Most fail to make use of the dozens of scientifically validated behaviour change strategies that exist. Behaviour change solutions are ignoring research, and behaviour change is framed the wrong way. It is still perceived as a chore.

Whether we are trying to lose weight, use less water, or save energy, positive behaviour change is unlikely to occur so long as it is perceived as a trade-off. Any desirable outcome that requires an immediate sacrifice of comfort remains wishful thinking if we fail to see beyond the hurdle. Implementing what we know that works is a logical necessity for effectively designing behaviour change. Without this, well-being is unlikely ever to appeal to a mainstream audience.

Good behaviour change approaches make life easier, not more complicated – recognising your progress, reminding you what you want, and facilitating your path to getting there. It could be a very promising angle for designing better behaviour change solutions. A lot of the successful emerging companies of the past decade or two have focused on helping us scratch our many itches. As Twitter and Medium co-founder Evan Williams summed up his recipe for success:

> *"Take a human desire, preferably one that has been around for a really long time... identify that desire and use modern technology to take out steps."*[2]

Quenching humanity's every desire does sound like heaven, but we all know it's more likely to resemble hell. As the surgeon-general (whoever that is) quoted on many alcohol bottles wisely dispenses: *drink in moderation* – and more importantly, *enjoy responsibly*. This is true for fermented beverages as much as it applies to life overall. Companies' obsession with giving us what we crave, instead of providing what we should instead be asking for, is slowly but steadily met by a more conscious revolution encouraging us to become our best selves through consumption in support of that ambition. The zeitgeist of the day, in fact, is developing an outright antagonism towards economic players looking to make a quick buck by creating ever-easier ways for us to succumb to common vices: companies inviting us to waste hours in our day glued to our screens, score great deals on pointless Internet purchases (my favourite of them all is an alarm clock combined with a coffee brewer, which is supposed to wake you up by brewing a cup of coffee – no joke!), and basically waste our life away procuring products and services that harm you as much as they harm the earth, but with the promise of luxury and bliss. As any scam artist knows, a scam is only as good as its audience *wanting to believe* it is real. I recently experienced this when booking a hotel that I intuitively knew would be subpar, simply because the deal advertised online looked *unreal.* It was a reminder of the good old adage: if it's too good to be true, it probably isn't.

Focus instead on originality and authentic value, as well as genuine care for our well-being. Our next trillion-dollar businesses will help us evolve towards a more mindful and sustainable existence, empowering and inspiring us to make purchases at a fair price and in ways that benefit all the actors involved. The upcoming age of consumption with a conscience respects human nature, Earth, and our personal struggles in resisting the ever-present temptation in favour of a disciplined, purposeful existence. They will help us be our best selves by focusing on the long-term outcome, instead of fleeting *fata morganas* of sky-high promises that no one is willing to be accountable for. And by being on the same side as their clientele, these businesses are creating a potent movement that will gradually and systematically reign supreme over the ugly, greedy, and fast-buck cult poisoning our commercial interactions with its destructive behaviour. Strong words, but *due words*.

> This is where the kale doughnut comes into play. The kale doughnut obviously isn't the latest the *deli* hype, but a metaphor for combining what you want now with what is good for you in the long run.

This is where the kale doughnut comes into play. The kale doughnut obviously isn't the latest the *deli* hype, but a metaphor for combining what you want now with what is good for you in the long run. It's the amalgamation of important, long-term needs kneaded in with a sprinkling of indulgent short-term wants. The alchemy of both is where truly winning propositions are forged. Whether you're an entrepreneur, public servant or corporate leader, embracing this is a winning recipe. In doing so, we can harmonise an errant, wants-centred hedonism with a wiser touch of care for ourselves and the world. Having a sense of purpose is the guiding light here, balancing pleasure and purpose optimally. Let's get ready for your future. There's no better way to kick this off than talking about a (purposeful) *future of work*.

Endnotes

1   https://ijbnpa.biomedcentral.com/articles/10.1186/s12966-014-0097-9

2   https://www.wired.com/2013/09/ev-williams-xoxo/

VI

IV

the future of work

" Being told what you're capable of
is fundamentally different from
experiencing it for yourself. "

Chapter 13

BECAUSE IT MATTERS
Rediscovering purpose

Imagine you are at a dinner party making conversation with the person next to you. Commonly, you will start by asking about what they do for a living; that is also the question you first expect from a stranger. Now, imagine said stranger answers as follows: *"I work in xyz, but to be honest, I only do it for the money..."* In most cases, it is unlikely that you will want to continue the conversation. On an interpersonal level, we have some degree of expectation that the people we interact with do what they do with a certain base level of purpose attached to it. Not so with corporations. Pretty much every corporation, since the invention of the legal entity itself, has openly and assertively declared its purpose to be the maximisation of profit (i.e., shareholder value). What is an acceptable goal for corporations is a poor answer on an interpersonal level. It's not surprising relational and transactional layers in business appear to coexist like oil and water, whereas they very much should be emulsified.

This observation is neither new nor particularly revolutionary. However, it is extremely important to realise the implications that it carries for our future. We've long treated human dynamics involved in our economic transactions as a sort of meta-layer of important but *unquantifiable* value creation activities, which fails to highlight how mission-critical they are. In reality, relationships are every bit as pivotal to our global business dealings as the capital systems enabling us to do what we do; both have coexisted for ages. Pretty much the same applies to our treatment of trust in business overall. We acknowledge its value in the absence of clarifying or quantifying its impact.

But digital is interweaving the transactional and relational layer in ways that traditional bureaucracy never could. Administrative legacy systems surviving to the present originate from the need to support a certain *type* of human collaboration until they eventually outlived their initial purpose. With ever more rapidly evolving needs, this administrative legacy has reached a point where it is doing more harm than good. All systems have the same Achilles' heel causing this to happen: once established, their primary concern is *maintaining the status quo and keeping their place* instead of serving the need they were built for.

All systems have the same Achilles' heel causing this to happen: once established, their primary concern is *maintaining the status quo and keeping their place* instead of serving the need they were built for.

Our economic interactions have always been dynamic and multifaceted (as is all complex collaboration) which explains why many of the legacy systems we still deal with today have been rendered inadequate. Digital systems replacing some of their paper-stamp ancestors are often much more flexible, allowing them to better respond to changing and evolving needs. Digital collaboration systems and platforms are also easier on humans, making much of the inter-human mediation we need to cooperate simpler, more convenient, and suitable to our nature and needs. On average, they're better designed for the task at hand – and designing for an intended purpose is by far their most important characteristic. On the surface, we face more pressure than ever to simplify our lives. Simultaneously, we deal with ever-greater complexity beneath the surface. The ensuing divide is to be somehow bridged. Systems and cultures must be built and nurtured to negotiate this tension.

Even under these circumstanced, a monolithic old-school bureaucratic administrative system can still be effective today if it is well designed. This is why some long-established organisations remain at the top of their game even in our modern world. But, on average, the nature of digital systems is far more suited to the current day and age – quite logically, because they evolved from it. The trust intermediation performed by a digital third-party typically requires less effort for everyone involved, streamlining value creation and delivery, as well as putting the people involved before the process. At least that is the promise offered by digital transformation programmes designed to reimagine how we interact. Overall, the key aspect for succeeding in this day and age is *adaptation* (i.e., an ability to dynamically respond to the many scenarios one might encounter). But adaptation must be more than holding your flag in the wind; it must go along clear directionality. Successful organisations do more than just adapt to whatever comes

> Some like the cliché that the only constant is change, but for the world's best organisations, the only constant is the purpose they continue to serve. What's constantly changing is the way in which they do it.

their way. They adapt in service of an overarching purpose that keeps them focused and on track. Some like the cliché that the only constant is change, but for the world's best organisations, the only constant is the purpose they continue to serve. What's constantly changing is the way in which they do it.

As humans, purpose has always mattered. To varying degrees, each and every one of us seeks meaning in how we live our lives. A large aspect of this endeavour revolves around our work. How we earn our living exerts significant influence on the way our lives unfold. The German word for *'profession'* literally translates to *'being called to do something'*, as is reflected by the English word 'vocation'. Semantically, one can be left to speculate whether this calling emerges from within or is assigned from the outside. The more purpose we find in our work, the more value we can surely generate from it. With capital as the dominant form of measuring this value generation, we traditionally view output firstly in economic terms. The content of our work plays a somewhat subordinate role in such an evaluation. That should surprise and concern us since the acquisition of financial means is not a wholesome purpose in itself.

Centuries after Adam Smith, Simon Sinek gave an illuminating talk on how much an employee-centric management culture can benefit a business and its ability to deliver customer value by telling the story of Noah.[1] In short, Sinek encountered a barista named Noah working in two hotels in Las Vegas. Sinek was impressed by the young employee's attitude, so he asked him whether he liked his job. "*I love my job,*" Noah replied. Intrigued by the answer, Sinek proceeded to asked what the hotel was doing to make Noah say so. Noah explained that throughout the day, *any* manager would stop by to see whether he needed assistance. Noah then mentioned that he also worked in another hotel, where managers stopped by only to check whether employees were doing the right thing and to catch misconduct. Noah said he would do all he could to keep his head low and stay under the radar in that environment. High-trust workplaces focusing on collaboration bring out the best in people, while low-trust workplaces struggle to manage away the worst. As Sinek concludes, the same individual is a completely different person depending on the workplace and the associated customer experience.[2]

> High-trust workplaces focusing on collaboration bring out the best in people, while low-trust workplaces struggle to manage away the worst.

Much of it boils down to leadership and attitude, which ultimately are shaped by the presence or absence or organisational purpose: in environments where people collectively work *towards* and *for* something, they waste less time on competing *against* each other in service of an agenda that serves only themselves. In organisations where lived purpose is lacking, people naturally proceed to focus on their own personal agendas. This effect is compounded by distrust because people receiving an attitude of distrust from colleagues and managers will respond with equal scepticism and start worrying about safeguarding their own interests in such a climate of latent hostility. Much distrust is, in fact, contagious.

If you're in a public place travelling with your luggage and you see other people holding on tightly to their luggage and behaving timid or concerned, you are likely to take similar efforts towards safeguarding your belongings. Now, what do you do if you have to go to the bathroom? Rather than trying to haul all your luggage around with you, you could ask a stranger to watch your things for you. But, do you trust them enough to do so? One notions of distrust – legitimate or not – infiltrate any human system, things become immediately more complicated. Purpose, even in such environments, gives us a reason to 'risk' trusting others. For instance, say you struck up a conversation with a person next to you and discovered that you are both die-hard fans of the same Korean drama. Sometimes the simple presence of shared preferences, beliefs, or values gives us enough confidence that someone is part of our *tribe* and, therefore, likely safe to trust. Purpose achieves this elegantly by creating common ground for the greatest number of people. It's a great strategy for aligning diverse and even large groups of people on a common denominator. Purpose allows us to feel well aligned whilst navigating our many individual differences, and this is why it's so powerful in keeping organisations focused and on track to perform. When purpose in an organisation is designed such that it further aligns internal interest with those of clients and other stakeholders, it's an excellent recipe for sustained success.

Shared belief in *something* means we operate as one and express value towards each other. It's evident that valued employees lead to valued customers because they emulate this gesture of trust and people-first philosophy towards those they are serving. In low-trust environments, the exact opposite happens with employees feeling encouraged to act in their own self-interest and distrust customers, especially when those are not satisfied. Fear of punishment for making concessions (i.e., refunding a disgruntled customer or remedying their experience at company cost) is destructive to the customer and employee experience alike. We've all been in situations that tell the story better than any principle can illustrate.

Organisations in a vicious cycle of distrust struggle more with delivering value, which further increases pressure on management to deliver results. As a result, you get heaps of unsustainable short-term focus, mutual blaming, and a general environment of hostility in which people do the bare minimum to get by. The virtuous cycle of trust-enabled and people-first culture makes every aspect of running organisations and delivering stakeholder value vastly easier. In an environment promoting relationships and trust, we have alignment through common ground, shared purpose, and a culture in which effective cooperation takes place. In organisations where this is lacking, individuals are incentivised to compete against each other instead of focusing on their organisation's value proposition and promise to the world.

Unfortunately, distrust can seem like the less risky choice. It is certainly the easier default state in an environment where capital reigns supreme, which explains many culture problems persisting in modern organisations today. Where capital takes centre stage, we can do business with people without having to like or trust them. But honestly, why would we want that any more than, say, *dating* people we neither like nor trust? Both are bad ideas if you're purpose-driven and looking for long-term well-being. Much of the dysfunctional management models that continue to survive today prevent businesses and people from reaching their full potential. It means purpose has been a marginalised topic in managerial thinking even though great leaders, since the beginning of time, have intuitively grasped its significance to any great achievement. Leadership is fundamentally about achieving something *with* others and only secondarily – if at all – about competing *against* someone. In a longitudinal study of 167 large corporations investigating the effects of leadership on sales, earnings, and profit margin, the authors found the former two variables significantly shaped by industry and company influences, whereas profit margin was most influenced by leadership.[3] This appears to suggest that organisations with effective leadership are the most profitable, which in turn suggests that people in such organisations are able to create greater value from the same resources compared to their peer benchmarks.

Often, great leadership makes up for shortcomings caused by corporate bureaucracy.[4] This is especially relevant during transformation efforts, as is purpose. A ship without a captain is a test of culture effectiveness, but a ship without direction is hopelessly lost. Modern organisations operating in the absence of leadership and purpose that are still able to deliver strong financial results just happen to be trawling particularly abundant fishing grounds – but those grounds may stop giving any time, and the destruction they leave in their wake is significant. Moreover, a well-steered boat discovering the same grounds will run rings around the trawler. The most talented people then proceed to jump ship and, all of a sudden, what used to be a mob of lucky pirates is rendered a bunch of starving sailors.

Leadership that effectively establishes purpose can focus on the important task at hand, and profit margins will naturally optimise. Like most desirable things in life, profit maximisation requires us to focus on something bigger so that it follows us, instead of forcing us to chase it. It requires optimism, courage, and trust in the direction being taken – but so does anything worth achieving. Putting money above all else, on the flipside, turns people bitter and makes them assume the worst in others. Money disputes are known to sabotage all kinds of human relationships, and obsession with the stuff easily creates emotional and moral desert land. Greed is adding nails to the collective human coffin. It would be better to salvage us from the kind of thinking that removes any reasonable distinction between us and our primate brethren.

Unfortunately, purpose is too often missed, especially when a pure financial lens is applied in analysing organisations. I vividly recall an argument with a bunch of hedge fund guys about what drives company value. They were convinced that cash flow told the entire story. The more that money infiltrates the human mind, the less alternative points of view it is comfortable to indulge. This isn't to say they were wrong and I was right, but it is to stress that money rarely questions itself. The statement that cash flow is the only significant aspect of a corporation is like saying sex is the only thing that matters in marriage.

Excellent service, competence, and insight into customer needs are the foundations that every successful business *needs* to build on. Whether it is able to capture all the value it creates for itself may very well be a question of margins, business acumen, and financial performance. It would be foolish to measure a business purely on those dimensions, however. Many businesses, especially small and family businesses, in general, exist today and will survive in the future because they are *purposeful endeavours* to the people behind them. And honestly speaking, what kind of world would we live in without them?

With its focus on high margins and lean organisations, many tech players epitomise the capitalist ideal of a successful business – but it often took years of high-profile losses to even get there. No wonder corporates across industries are excited to emulate it and transform into *'technology companies'.* All of that is understandable, but sadly misses the point entirely. Technology is a formidable *amplifier* with which *great value propositions* can be delivered and scaled effectively. No company can rely on technology and financials alone. Human capital is essential to delivering any worthwhile proposition, old or new economy. Scale, in this conversation, is not a holy grail, but a matter of choice. A small business owner may prefer to run her business on a proudly small scale, and be content with that. A growth-orientated entrepreneur may instead choose to focus on building for scale, and potentially accepting large-scale losses in the process. The rewards of such an endeavour can be truly massive – every scaled business is an opportunity to make a dent in the world by changing the way things are done. Many brick-and-mortar businesses can become very profitable at extreme scale, *exactly like* nearly every technology company. But as is true for our small business owner, ambitions for scale don't always work out – something we notice especially in the tech sector. Many buoyantly funded tech companies don't *even* become profitable *when* they reach extreme scale.

Small- and large-scale preferences both have downsides. Small-scale businesses are limited in resources and reach. Large-scale players are limited by the restrictions that come with growth capital, and often by internal alignment and decision-making issues. That's always been the case. What's truly interesting, though, is how both worlds have become highly interwoven through the advent of platform economy business models. Technology companies building scaled digital intermediaries for us to get a variety of things done rely on small business to be platform inventory. This illustrates a phenomenon that has always been true, but is now becoming more obvious than ever: We need entrepreneurs focusing on big horizons as much as we need those hawking goods and services independently and on a small scale. It's surely rewarding to build technology companies intermediating trust and value between people and goods or services, but that activity would be entirely worthless if it weren't for the countless people and small businesses performing the *actual* value creation activities behind it. And what will our world be like when those businesses cease to exist? Your chosen search engine could never replace the local greengrocer or give you a charming neighbourhood bar. Much of the digital economy wouldn't exist were it not for their offline partners running said small businesses. Our world would be a pretty sad place without entrepreneurs driven by something other than scale, margins and monopolistic growth obsessions. Unsurprisingly, most of these are strings attached to growth capital.

On the flipside, many technology companies are doing truly extraordinary things that genuinely benefit humanity – and the reason they do is, once again, purpose. Telling start-ups built on the sole purpose of scoring their founders a huge exit apart from those finding real purpose in solving an important problem is extremely easy: the former rarely live up to their hype, while the latter more often than not become household names. As the saying goes, the best way to do well is to do something others want to see you succeed at. Purpose-driven businesses don't look down on their peers; they uplift whoever they have the chance interact with. The best businesses, tech or otherwise, make it their job to empower the people in and around them.

Some of the intangible value in those many pursuits may not be imminently (or ever) measurable in capital terms, but that value still very much exists. And even when we look at *tangible* examples of value creation, purpose-driven companies outperform their peers by a wide margin (and probably have a lot more fun doing it). The *intrinsic* value of purpose-driven work is far more multifaceted than its extrinsic rewards as measured in terms of capital, margins, and scale. Were it not for *purpose-driven* individuals, there would be few extraordinary brands or inspirational success stories. There'd also be few great restaurants, hotels, or bars, and certainly not much art. The world would miss many amenities that make life pleasant and interesting. I am deeply grateful that we haven't reached this point just yet.

> Even when we look at *tangible* examples of value creation, purpose-driven companies outperform their peers by a wide margin (and probably have a lot more fun doing it). The *intrinsic* value of purpose-driven work is far more multifaceted than its extrinsic rewards as measured in terms of capital, margins, and scale.

A *Harvard Business Review* article on *"Creating a Purpose-Driven Organization"* by Robert Quinn and Anjan Thakor, makes the case for purpose as clear as day, telling the story of *DTE*, an energy company focused solely on shareholder returns. In the face of low employee engagement and the 2008 Financial Crisis, CEO Garry Anderson opened up to an idea proposed by one of his board members whose credo was that a leader ought *'to connect people to their purpose?* Anderson decided to give it a try by celebrating his employees' contribution to the community in a way that staff

felt was authentic and moving, kicking off an internal transformation
of the most impactful kind:

> *"The company received a Gallup Great Workplace Award for*
> *five years in a row. And financial performance responded in*
> *kind: DTE's stock price more than tripled from the end of 2008*
> *to the end of 2017."*[6]

The authors of the article also take the standpoint that viewing
employees as self-interested agents is somewhat a self-fulfilling
prophecy, causing the very problems many managers are afraid of.
They also advise caution in articulation of a purpose to ensure it is
real and effective. In their words:

> *"You do not invent a higher purpose; it already exists. You can*
> *discover it through empathy—by feeling and understanding*
> *the deepest common needs of your workforce. That involves*
> *asking provocative questions, listening, and reflecting."*[7]

But ambition and reality have yet to properly align. *"79% of business
leaders believe that purpose is central to business success and to an
organization's existence; yet, only 34% agree that purpose is a
guidepost for leadership decision-making. This gap demonstrates the
optimism and promise that leaders see in being purpose-driven to
elevate business, but a hesitation to "walk-the-walk" and actively
embed it into foundational elements of the company, such as
organizational decision architecture."*[8] Still, a survey among
executives asked to rank the most important factors organisations
used to evaluate annual performance found *societal impact* to be
the top factor, before *customer satisfaction, financial performance*,
and *employee satisfaction and retention.*[9] Among surveyed leaders,
they identified a group that exemplified a *"doing good is good
business"* mantra and found them to be generally more inclined

to invest in disruptive technologies, more ethically aware, and more rigorous in their decision-making.

Many of the world's highest-performing organisations are now beginning to reinvigorate their cultures with a strong sense of purpose. For pioneers like *Unilever,* this has paid off extraordinarily. As the company explains in a press release, its *"purpose-led, Sustainable Living Brands are growing 69% faster than the rest of the business and delivering 75% of the company's growth."*[10] This renewed focus on purpose goes hand in hand with a wholesome approach to value creation which seeks to make value chains more equitable and sustainable. Many people already make consumption decisions *"based on how brands treat their people, how they treat the environment and how they support the community in which they operate."*[11] As these influencing factors have become more and more understood, they are driving a tectonic shift in management thinking.

Putting purpose before profit as a core organisational pursuit is likely to bring with it countless tangible and intangible advantages. Technology sure has a big role to play here, but it's not a purpose in itself. Well-chosen purpose can fix much of what's broken in organisations – whether big or small within the old or new economy. However optimistic or sceptical you are about the growing role of organisational purpose, a corresponding transition from shareholder to stakeholder capitalism is already well on its way to becoming a *global macrotrend*, and well worth taking a close look at.

Endnotes

1   https://www.youtube.com/watch?v=RyTQ5-SQYT0
2   https://www.youtube.com/watch?v=vc4FEIYvkQc

3   https://www.jstor.org/stable/2094020?seq=1

4   www.emeraldinsight.com/0969-6474.htm

5   https://hbr.org/2018/07/creating-a-purpose-driven-organization

6   Ibid.

7   Ibid.

8   https://www.pwc.com/us/en/about-us/corporate-responsibility/assets/pwc-putting-purpose-to-work-purpose-survey-report.pdf

9   https://www2.deloitte.com/content/dam/Deloitte/global/Documents/gx-davos-DI_Success-personified-fourth-industrial-revolution.pdf

10 https://www.unilever.com/news/press-releases/2019/unilevers-purpose-led-brands-outperform.html

11 https://www2.deloitte.com/us/en/insights/topics/marketing-and-sales-operations/global-marketing-trends/2020/purpose-driven-companies.html

Chapter 14

SO MUCH AT STAKE
Transitioning to stakeholder capitalism

I n August of last year, an eminent association of chief executives representing corporate America issued a statement in which they sought to redefine the goal of a corporation. Here is an excerpt:

> *"While each of our individual companies serves its own corporate purpose, we share a fundamental commitment to all of our stakeholders. We commit to:*
>
> - *Delivering value to our customers. We will further the tradition of American companies leading the way in meeting or exceeding customer expectations.*
> - *Investing in our employees. This starts with compensating them fairly and providing important benefits. It also includes supporting them through training and education*

that help develop new skills for a rapidly changing world.
We foster diversity and inclusion, dignity, and respect.
- *Dealing fairly and ethically with our suppliers. We are*
  dedicated to serving as good partners to the other companies,
  large and small, that help us meet our missions.
- *Supporting the communities in which we work. We respect*
  the people in our communities and protect the environment
  by embracing sustainable practices across our businesses.
- *Generating long-term value for shareholders, who provide*
  the capital that allows companies to invest, grow and
  innovate. We are committed to transparency and effective
  engagement with shareholders. "[1]

But it may well be a case of *back to the future.* Many organisations decades before this already knew the value of defining and living an inclusive purpose. I'd go even as far to say that great businesses started with a strong sense of purpose. Many modern-day insurance corporations, for instance, were born from so-called *mutuals* – organisations of merchants associating for the purpose of sharing risk among their community. Fast forward to today, and it's fair to say organisations need simply to be reminded of their purpose and stakeholder responsibilities so they're able to create value in a more balanced, sustainable, and effective way.

Indeed, some global players can look upon a long history of expressing and standing by their societal contribution. In 1943, Johnson & Johnson published their values statement, aptly titled *"Our Credo."* In abbreviation:

"We believe our first responsibility is to the patients, doctors
and nurses, to mothers and fathers and all others who use our
products and services. (...) Our business partners must have

an opportunity to make a fair profit. (...) We are responsible to our employees who work with us throughout the world. (...) We are responsible to the communities in which we live and work and to the world community as well. We must help people be healthier by supporting better access and care in more places around the world. We must be good citizens — support good works and charities, better health and education, and bear our fair share of taxes. We must maintain in good order the property we are privileged to use, protecting the environment and natural resources. (...) Our final responsibility is to our stockholders. Business must make a sound profit. (...) When we operate according to these principles, the stockholders should realize a fair return."

Note how in both examples above, shareholder and stockholder value respectively are mentioned *last* in the list, and the adjective *"long-term"* has been added to signify that this is not about chasing quarterly figures, but about value generation for society. There is now mainstream evidence of a gradual move towards understanding corporate purpose as more than being self-centred profit machines corresponding to Adam Smith's ideology. Whether an organisation makes this happen on a PR or operational level will vary, but it illustrates a clear linkage between corporations and their contribution to overall socio-economic well-being whose future importance will certainly grow further. This connection has mostly been implied by a majority; now it is being made explicit. The story of economic selfishness creating collective benefit has been widely exposed as a fairy tale, giving us room to paint a more accurate picture.

Considering the eclectic workforce of many multinational organisations and five generations working alongside – and sometimes colliding with – each other in the workplace, we are achieving an astonishing amount of diversity.[2] Whether that becomes a company's greatest asset or remains an Achilles' heel really depends on how much of a *shared foundation and purpose* they are able to establish across the organisation. More than ever, managing this larger and more diverse set of stakeholders needs a new take. Corporations must seek a healthy dialogue based on commonality with all of their stakeholders. Building such common ground gives everyone involved better reasons to collaborate over competing, resulting in greater shared benefit and much less dysfunctional conflict to achieve it. It allows corporations to benefit from all stakeholder interaction instead of feeling an urge to *manage* those touchpoints in a certain way. Generally, the nature of interactions is far more constructive when parties involved are working towards a horizon of mutual gain instead of *compromise.*

> Generally, the nature of interactions is far more constructive when parties involved are working towards a horizon of mutual gain instead of *compromise.*

Unifying and responding to the needs of many eclectic stakeholders may seem like an unsurmountable and complex challenge when approached with conventional thinking. And indeed, our thinking and the problem-solving strategies we deploy must adapt for the better. An interesting piece by former Rotman School of Management Dean Roger Martin explains how it can work. After interviewing dozens of exemplary leaders, he believed them to share a trait which he termed *"integrative thinking:"* the ability to *"hold in their heads to two opposing ideas at once".*[3]

This skill, according to Martin, allows some of the most successful executives and CEOs to find *consensus beyond compromise*, discovering solutions that creatively resolve the tension between opposing perspectives. These individuals are able to chart an inclusive way forward in which everyone feels accommodated and listened to. Such leaders, unlike their less exemplary peers, embrace diversity and multiple perspectives without taking sides, but instead with a determination to unite them into wholesome (i.e., *integrative*) solutions, satisfying the greatest number of people in the best possible way.[4] Using creative problem-solving, they find universally appreciated solutions: *"Integrative thinkers embrace complexity, tolerate uncertainty, and manage tension in searching for creative solutions to problems."*[5] It's a simple yet powerful trick. By focusing their energy and attention on discovering commonality dissonance becomes an asset and an opportunity for unexpected ideas to emerge. If politicians were skilled integrative thinkers, we probably wouldn't have all that much conflict – and if all the world's managers followed suit, we'd have ourselves a dramatically better business world.

But is it really that easy to turn disagreement into innovation? Martin's research shows that many of the most successful leaders share this uniquely advantageous trait.[6]

Our global economic and political systems, almost needless to say, are not geared towards facilitating integrative problem solving. Administration systems tend to become their own centre of the universe – the more bureaucratic, the more prominent this effect – and thus reinforce the mental models used to create them. Often times, the clash of mental models occurring when two

> The clash of mental models occurring when two different, seemingly incompatible systems collide is the real hurdle and not so much the *underlying reality* these systems are describing.

different, seemingly incompatible systems collide is the real hurdle and not so much the *underlying reality* these systems are describing. Separating reality from how it is perceived is already quite an effort in conversation with others, but it is nigh on impossible when the said view is reinforced by decades or even centuries of administrative legacy.

All systems serve to simplify things for us, and they do it by establishing a certain perspective on reality. We often cannot resist to succumb to status quo blindness. Much of this is implied in the way a system works. For example, a permanently open subway ticket gantry implies an assumption that most people carry a valid commuter card or ticket, such that gantry would only need to close in exceptional circumstances. Compared to a gantry that opens only on validation, the open gantry approach (as seen in the Tokyo underground system) reduces energy usage and wear and tear on the gantry whilst ensuring faster transit through the gate. It also makes for a more pleasant user experience. Perhaps you are inclined to overlook such details, but instead you should take note how they tell a pretty meaningful story.

Something as simple as the above implicitly communicates a worldview according to which the average person is viewed as considerate, honest, and responsible. The Japanese are a quintessential example of a high-interpersonal trust society, which in other cultures would be considered an explicit invitation for anarchy. High-trust environments like these operate differently than their low-trust equivalents, and the signals are seen everywhere if one is attuned to them. Something as simple as a subway gantry, jointly with countless other artefacts of everyday living (unintentionally), communicates its take on humanity and the world. In contexts that expect people to behave like adults and self-regulate, they more often than not do just that. A gantry designed with the mental model that people are *generally dutiful and can be trusted to behave correctly* is, of course, mirrored by a society exemplifying this. Such a subway gantry system is a showcase of the *'minimum viable distrust'* strategy I mentioned earlier. Compare this to the usual subway gantry, which is more of an *enforcement machine*. It remains closed until riders prove their innocence by flashing a valid ticket or metro card. In this context, the gantry is metaphorical for ideal versus current stakeholder relations in many organisations. At present, most companies keep the gantry closed, assuming the view that stakeholders need be managed so as to avert any potential for damage. In the new model of stakeholder capitalism, that gantry is opened to enable a smoother and more streamlined interaction.

Maximum viable trust is an excellent principle on which to build stakeholder engagement and dialogue. Naturally, societies with high levels of inter-societal trust tend to prefer operating on *'maximum viable trust'* supported by governance mechanisms guided by an approach of *'minimum viable distrust'.* One of the pressing issues making a shift to stakeholder capitalism absolutely necessary is the current challenge of harmonising long-term and short-term business objectives. Most companies choose one. Predictably so, publicly listed corporations get caught up in chasing quarters and potentially losing sight of the end game. Notable exceptions to this are a handful of successful tech companies whose share value has risen exponentially independent of earnings.

On the incumbent side, Paul Polman was one of the few pioneers who believed in shifting organisations away from obsessive short-term thinking. Famously within his first day on the job as CEO of

Unilever, he abolished quarterly reporting. When we had a chat about it in 2015 at the St. Gallen Symposium, he was adamant that it was the right direction for big companies to take. His actions displayed the kind of courage you wish every c-Suite leader had. In his own words: *"The first day I became CEO, I stopped guidance. I figured the first day they hire you, they're not going to fire you."*[7]

This goes to show just how against the grain something as sensible as overcoming excessive short-term orientation seems to be in corporates that are unduly obsessed with their shareholders. But I also feel a need to express caution over focusing exclusively on the long-term. Many organisations have been doing so for quite some time, but that alone doesn't make them role models. Sure, it's great when a business is in it for the long haul. However, that isn't enough to make a company truly stand out anymore. Some governments have notably been very good at long-term thinking, and certainly Singapore and Japan are the North Star examples here. That doesn't necessarily mean that this long-term strategic planning is equally effective in addressing pressing issues and disruptive shifts today. Notably, Singapore would also be an example for a country with a progressive innovation strategy which transforms public service on an ongoing basis. Long-term and short-term planning go hand and hand when they are purposeful, centred around solving meaningful problems and holistic in nature.

This is true in the same way for companies who must find ways of connecting their strategic direction with what's going on in the lives of the people they impact. On some level, that is called customer experience, but, on many other levels, it links back to the ability of communicating and operationalising a strong sense of purpose. Generally, this direction will be simple and compelling, enabling everyone to individually make sense of it in a way best suited to them. As we have discovered, when purpose is built into organisations, it's a powerful cultural and behavioural anchor, gathering everyone on common ground and focusing the organisation to naturally align. This transforms an organisation into an organism with a focused and worthy direction. Such a degree of focal specialisation is the natural answer to what industrial thinking was trying to achieve with its cult and directive of efficiency: maximising the potential of all organisational inputs to generate the greatest possible output. The difference is that when purpose sets this direction, it's actually fun for those involved, and a great guiding principle for finding good balance between short- and long-term thinking, investment, and progress.

Where industrialism made us believe that we had to choose between purpose and profit maximisation, as well as between personal fulfilment and gainful employment, the age of stakeholder capitalism is distinctly of view that these objectives can be integrated into one overarching philosophy. It's the best and perhaps soon will be the only way of governing organisations properly. In a world too complex for template approaches or rigid processes to be effective, common ground is precious real estate. Managerial styles in which folks are told what to do, *what to think*, and how to blindly follow will at best be a

> Where industrialism made us believe that we had to choose between purpose and profit maximisation, as well as between personal fulfilment and gainful employment, the age of stakeholder capitalism is distinctly of view that these objectives can be integrated into one overarching philosophy.

compromise and at worst lead to organisations' demise. We'll need a new take on organisational structure and governance.

We will witness a much more distributed decision-making process, responding with agility to what's going on in the immediate context. It's practically necessary in order to move forward and maintain a winning pace in this eclectic and fast-changing world we live in. What we already know is that the existing corporate stakeholder model requires reinvention. The only reason many organisations still perform fairly and decently is that people on the inside and external economic conditions on the outside can make up for the frictions caused by systems no longer fit for operation in the current environment. But these businesses could create much more value from their existing resources and inputs than they currently are by embracing structural, managerial, and cultural transformation. The problem is such lost opportunity cost is usually invisible. But imagine the positive impact of structures purpose-built to galvanise us, so we can do our best work and mint all of it into maximum stakeholder value. How much greater a contribution would it be able to make?

Re-engineering business to generate exponentially more value, and then to take a more equal approach to distributing that value, will benefit us all in the long run. More wholesome and equal focus on all of the relevant stakeholders in an organisation will make things fairer – especially for those who have thus far received only the shavings of wealth generation. They should, by all means, get their fair share going forward. Surely you can't run a business without a CEO, but you most definitely can't run a business without a frontline. And while, say, a branded luxury product is about the customer experience and its origin story, it wouldn't come to be without the ingredients or the people making it. Stakeholder-focused capitalism is an admission of wrongs worth righting such that socio-economic growth can be as inclusive as possible.

Economies with a distinctive middle-class spread already tend to fare better in this area; for example, many nations in Scandinavia and Western Europe tend to have greater social equality that rewards diverse professions more equally and fairly. Needless to say, no form of state has yet to truly succeed in achieving perfect overarching social equality. Looking at the distributed social governance we see in many places within digital economy platforms could very well be a source of innovation in this area.

In such environments, naturally emerging reciprocity and mutual gain are often easy to come by. The community flourishes because everybody is encouraged to contribute their best. What we see here is that a kind of *contextual capitalism* where people collaborate for financial and social capital gains, without a desire for gaining more than others, is prevalent. This typically works very frictionlessly and on the basis of dialogue. In this environment, a productive engagement model for stakeholder capitalism occurs naturally. As our younger generations inherit the task to reinvent corporations for a brighter future we can expect a greater and faster pace of change going forward.

Endnotes

1   https://www.businessroundtable.org/business-roundtable-redefines-the_purpose_of-a-corporation-to-promote-an-economy-that-serves-all-americans

2   https://hbr.org/2014/09/managing-people-from-5-generations

3   https://hbr.org/2007/06/how-successful-leaders-think

4 https://rogerlmartin.com/docs/default-source/Articles/integrative-thinking/the-art-of-integrative-thinking

5 Ibid.

6 https://store.hbr.org/product/becoming-an-integrative-thinker-the-keys-to-success/ROT051

7 https://www.washingtonpost.com/news/on-leadership/wp/2015/05/21/the-tao-of-paul-polman/

Chapter 15

VALUE GENERATION
Intergenerational workplace challenges

The conflict between older and younger generations is as old as humanity. Generation Z, or centennials in popular parlance, may puzzle us greatly, yet we can expect to learn as much from them as they from us. Like no generation before them, centennials' childhoods were mostly dominated by a strange mix of apocalyptic global events, as well as the luxuries of ubiquitous technology and generous parenting. My take is that Gen Z, much unlike many emerging generations of people, isn't preoccupied *primarily* with rebellion, but comes instead with an almost depressing realism towards the dysfunctional nature of the status quo and the insufficiency of systems we rely on to govern humanity. They also seem particularly attuned to the strange incompatibility and coexistence of the old and new world, cultivating an almost fatalistic sense of self-irony on the one hand

and a strong awareness and drive to make use of the endless possibilities granted by technology on the other. All of this is purely anecdotal, based on my conversations among friends and acquaintances of this generation. However we may sketch the Gen Z archetype, what matters most is recognising just how much they, as any generation, are a product of the zeitgeist. Their struggles, perspectives, and virtues give us a new lens to perceive what's wrong with the way things are and how they could be instead.

A tumultuous conflict unfolds in how different generations make sense of and own their digital alter egos. For Gen Zs, and to a certain extent Gen Ys, digital is the equivalent of reality. It's the default with which to make sense of the world. What many young people seem to intuitively know is that many of the societal conventions we still rely upon today aren't just outdated, but wildly conflicting with the reality of our digital selves. Whilst we've seen daily life impacted by technology in all facets, its impact on reshaping essential administrative systems has been surprisingly shallow in many places. Sure, we've digitised paper forms. But, the very bureaucracy upon which modern society rests has been subject to close to zero innovation. Generations that grew up in ages where paper-stamp bureaucracy was the standard in all aspects of life may not have any real issues with this. For those of us who grew with the promise of technology streamlining all aspects of life might find this inadequate. Simplicity, convenience, and flexibility of technology is perhaps considered an optional luxury by generations who grew up without it, but not so by those reared in these very comforts. Raised to expect these benefits across all aspects of life, and reluctant to put up with needlessly cumbersome legacies, this generation is resentful about the discrepancy between what already is possible versus what is in many places a sorely outdated status quo.

In my opinion, this means that the emerging generations of today aren't rebelling against the system for the sake of it or demanding anarchy as an alternative. Instead, knowing all the possibilities modern technology and digital infrastructure offers them, they are simply unwilling to accept a socio-economic reality in which these possibilities have not been taken advantage of. They just believe there's a more convenient and often better way – and they are right about that. The problem is that digital existence has blurred the lines between what's real and artificial so much that it makes rules and delineations seem arbitrary. In this as in many other cases, the only true solution is reinforcing the value of ethics and our collective human conscience, unless we really do desire the digital economy to give us a permanent escape from reality, without ever becoming a meaningful way to run our societies at large. Many people are already addicted to the dopamine rush of the instant gratification they can obtain from the Internet. Other than making us perpetually yearn for more, technology that scratches the itch isn't competent enough to provide us with a sensibly digitised existence. Technology must align with our long-term goals to help us achieve the meaningful. The kind of companies doing that will be a different beast to those focused on making us spend as much of our waking hours on our screens, so that they can serve us advertisements for things we don't need.

While digital technology could be the most promising bridge between generations – helping us all live more delightfully and understand each other better – it could also be our collective demise. Widespread digital adoption may replace legacy systems, but it should avoid indiscriminately displacing values that serve an important purpose in our surroundings. Separating the underlying social context from the (outdated) solution will be essential for us to preserve worthy traditions and social dynamics whilst dramatically modernising the rails society operates on. Like many centennials and millennials (yes, we all hate that word) teach their grandparents how to create lip sync videos, emerging generations must also value an exchange in the other direction, without spam-filtering it as irrelevant or archaic. Humanity will only evolve for the better if we know how to distinguish between the social fibre worth preserving and exhausted legacies worth decommissioning. In a world where perception, reality, and context are increasingly blending, we must relearn to distinguish this new perspective. Then, and perhaps only then, we will be able to facilitate a more productive multilateral dialogue between the generations.

Gen Y and *Z* increasingly and indiscriminately trust technology because it makes life easier. *Gen Alpha* – the youngest of the bunch, born between mid-2010s and 2020s – will likely exacerbate this trend, and inadvertently add their own spin to it. Meanwhile *Baby Boomers* and *Gen X* are more sceptical and resist this somewhat. This is the difference between the digital natives and the digital aliens. That disconnect between generations is likely to escalate. More senior generations expect trust to be earned; young folks trust instantly and expect to be trusted by default (until or unless they mess up). This already causes significant frustration within organisations; different generations have different attitudes to trust as well as data, technology, and leadership. Misunderstandings arising from this can become a dysfunctional blame game of *'why don't you trust me'* versus *'why don't you work towards earning my trust'*. Both are right, in a way. Too much and too little default trust are equally detrimental. The trust-first camp will over-trust and take far too high of risks until (in the worst case) everything comes crashing down. Where too much scepticism hurts digital adoption, digital carelessness also hinders meaningful progress. Both behaviours reinforce each other and are equally dysfunctional. Just think of the prolific cybersecurity issues we already have today! Meanwhile, companies and people who embrace distrust as their first principle will keep adding more rules to their world until it becomes impossible to operate, let alone compete. That world will eventually grind to a halt, suffocated by its own bureaucracy.

The distrust epidemic in the old economy and over-trust epidemic in the new economy quite bizarrely co-exist. Many of us inevitably live across both these worlds. Complicated by intergenerational trust dynamics and attitudes, it leaves humanity scattered in search of a unifying and balanced approach to harmonise these extremes. Finding our common ground amidst all this may take time, but is a worthwhile pursuit. As we explored prior, being on the same page requires us to look past individual preferences – and focus on mutual perspectives that enhance the greater good.

Much speaks for finding a middle path. We've looked at how smart organisations are starting to realise that such a common ground across their diversity is possible. That turns diversity into a genuine business asset rather than additional complexity to manage.

When it comes to intergenerational dialogue, we must distinguish between universal values worthy of keeping and individual opinions getting in the way of common understanding. Both are a function of the society we live in. A British grandfather may want Brexit and a British Millennial may want the legalisation of cannabis. It's pretty difficult to build any common ground on those simple attitudes, for they will likely spark hostility and misunderstanding between the two. This brings us back to the conversation on wants versus needs. Wants, as we have found, are far more diverse, yet far less significant in terms of reflecting our world. This really means discovering common ground must focus on the needs. A world focused on wants likes to pretend humans are too different to get along with each other. This is also the story of intergenerational dissonance. At a needs level, it's a deceptive illusion. We will realise equality and harmony by remembering that we are all made of the same fabric, irrespective of generation and other identities defining us. This understanding will allow us to excavate fruitful mutual understanding – and perhaps even appreciation – at global, societal, organisational, and interpersonal levels, enabling greater trust, lesser friction, and a much more harmonious socio-economic co-existence. If intergenerational conflict teaches us one thing, it's that we must urgently

> If intergenerational conflict teaches us one thing, it's that we must urgently stop misunderstanding each other and shift to a worldview in which effective interhuman communication co-exists with its diversity.

stop misunderstanding each other and shift to a worldview in which effective interhuman communication co-exists with its diversity. Generations shape our identity and behaviour. In this regard, they are symbolic of all other influence factors shaping humanity.

Chapter 16

LEADING WITH AGILITY
A new take on leadership and organisational structure

Agility and *agile transformation* have likely overtaken *innovation* as the most abused and least practised buzzword in business today. Why agility is misunderstood and mangled is a bit of a mystery. For starters, many people still believe agility is a method. Agility is an actionable way of referring to strategy and culture rooted in the *Agile Manifesto*. In only 68 words, it delineates the principles for effective software development. These principles have since become general guidelines for a new way of work. The ideas contained in it are absolutely valid beyond the field of software. But like many things that have been excessively glorified, the hype typically distracts attention away from the original idea, in pursuit of commercialising it in the most rigorous manner.

As a result, countless people around the world are being given the impression that agility is some kind of magic bullet method for achieving anything in any kind of environment. But it's a tad more complicated in my eyes. Agile organisations are great because they enable high-performance and are superbly well-run – not because they've heard of the *Agile Manifesto* or follow it word-by-word. In fact, agility simply refers to a mindset that *enables* a type of collaborative environment in which the best possible results for stakeholders can be achieved. Organisations that have put in place a purpose-built structure to support this kind of thinking and culture are likely to thrive. But agility is incompatible with organisations suffering from dysfunctional, excessively political, and internally misaligned leadership and people. In those environments, however great the ambition to become 'agile', the results will backfire or, at best, lead to absolutely zero betterment whatsoever.

> Agility is incompatible with organisations suffering from dysfunctional, excessively political, and internally misaligned leadership and people.

Many organisations, therefore, come face to face with the challenges in operationalising agile transformation. This is just another way of saying that their current culture is so distanced from agile ways of working that any attempt at shifting towards this new approach would likely fail in practice. What happens instead in these organisations is that agile tools are being implemented as if they were equivalent to the agile mindset. This may mean that people use new work technologies or stand-up meetings as a way of enacting a scenario in which something has actually changed. Such agile *'implementation'* typically has zero impact. Rather, it frustrates the people involved because they might be wondering why this so-called *'agile transformation'* hasn't yielded any tangible benefits in their work environments.

When we understand agile culture, we must appreciate all of its dimensions, not just the very common understanding that agility is about openness to change plans. Agility prioritises *people over process, work delivered over work documented, collaboration over negotiation, and responsiveness to change over following a predefined plan.* It's equally important to resist the temptation of disqualifying methods as non-agile because non-agility is mostly a function of behaviour. It's less about what tools you use and more about *how* you use them. It's about getting comfortable with the idea of moving goalposts without letting those distract from achieving real progress. It's also about the responsibility instilled in every individual, entrusted with taking ownership of their work and figuring out how to reach the desired destination in their best possible way. A heavily method-centric conversation about agility is actually missing the point. Transforming the culture in which work gets done matters way more to the outcome.

The more flexibly we view the operational aspects of agility, the more versatile and easier it becomes to implement in various environments. This also applies to how we interface with stakeholders that we would consider non-agile in approach and their requirements for say predictability and documentation of our planning and work. Such interfaces, especially between teams of people who work in different ways, define the modern work world. With this, there's no point in force-feeding a method to all your stakeholders just because you (or your c-suite) work that way. Agile transformation succeeds when we stop abusing the concept and start focusing on ways to meet everyone's needs.

Agility should, thus, be seen as an organisational philosophy for the digital age, much like design thinking. Transformation towards agility is actually happening in the heads of the people; tools then help translate that into new routines. I like to visualise this in form of an *agility pyramid* of fundamentals, building neatly on top of each other:

The Agility Pyramid

6. Data enables great performance

5. Technology enables great data (insights)

4. Systems enable great technology (solutions)

3. Talent enables great systems

2. Culture enables great talent

1. Purpose enables great culture

The foundation of this agility pyramid, the place where we all start, is purpose. This is what it takes to align people. Unlike what you may have been told, alignment is not making people agree with you; it's inspiring them to act in a certain way of their own accord. Imagine a chiropractor or a physiotherapist. Adjusting is an important part of the treatment, but a good practitioner will always recommend behaviour changes, such as becoming more aware of your posture and doing exercises that help you uphold the positive change that the adjustment brings in the long-term. You'll probably do that only if you are motivated to do something good for yourself and trust their medical advice, and if you personally see meaning in it. In other words, you must believe in it in order to behave in line with it.

Forcing alignment is painful and naïve because the improvement will not last beyond the intervention. Purpose builds and adjusts culture; culture is basically how things get done. Culture itself doesn't answer the why because culture is an ever evolving and adapting phenomenon. It simply is what it is. What culture is great at is guaranteeing a certain kind of behaviour. Given a choice between relying on an elaborate contract or a human cultural convention to ensure something takes place, I'd place my bet on culture. Culture is probably the only thing in the world that achieves close to 100% compliance without a standardised rule book or the need for any enforcement beyond social dynamics. Cultural standards are socialised, largely implicit, and passed on through behaviours. Formal texts describe culture, but they don't *define* it. Culture is complex, and so is the world it exists in. Its dynamic nature and *ability to establish common ground among even very large groups of people* is remarkable. So is its versatility and openness to internal or external influences, allowing it to assume countless faces and provide meaning for a vast range of people it encircles. This all transpires while maintaining a mutual connection and shared identity. But because culture serves to find commonality among diverse groups of individuals, it is also inherently status quo biased. Culture is often questioned, but rarely are questions immediately met with enthusiasm. All of us exist within cultures. This is something we take for granted. Our implicit or explicit association with cultural circles of various shapes and sizes is a reality that we operate in daily. However liberal you like to be with the definition, one could argue that anything from, say, someone's yoga routine to their job in HR, family heritage, and meme preferences is indicative of belonging to certain cultural circles.

The nature of culture demonstrates the inherent agility of humanity and cultural concepts in themselves, but also shows the power of status quo bias. When you join a stamp collector community, you will feel automatically compelled to align with the often unspoken conventions and mental models of that group. These tend to find expression in language. Perhaps you've noticed that certain groups like gamers and surgeons have their own *'secret language'* with which they communicate on an axis of belonging to the same circle. Dialects from *Singlish* to *Frisian* (and anything in between) are essentially the same. Quite remarkably, we don't need formal definitions of all these behavioural cues in order to follow them to great effect. Humanity is *inherently agile.*

> Humanity is *inherently agile.* It explains how high alignment can be achieved between vastly heterogenous groups of people.

It explains how high alignment can be achieved between vastly heterogenous groups of people without necessarily much bureaucracy. Shared trust in a purpose we're interested in enables us to perceive common ground and use our innate ability for agility towards it.

When in place, you will notice how people begin to approach work like their hobbies or passions: with much dedication and motivation. No code of conduct alone can inspire such proactiveness. Policies are limited to get us to *react* to something in a certain way, but they're hopeless in making us *proactive.* Yet proactiveness is, of course, necessary in high-level problem-solving and peak performance. The best organisations actively identify problems, instead of just reacting to full-on fires with emergency interventions. Rules are more or less decent at making people comply, but they are terrible at inspiring us to do what's right because we believe it to be so. Anybody who believes that a world as complex as today's can be adequately governed with rules alone is in denial. In the famous words of Antoine de Saint-Exupéry:

> *"If you want to build a ship, don't drum up the men to gather wood, divide the work, and give orders. Instead, teach them to yearn for the vast and endless sea."*

Saint-Exupéry passed in 1944 and yet here we are in the 2020s with the vast majority of people still believing orders, materials, and ages are all it takes to build a solid ship. Agile transformation involves decommissioning mental models of rule-based domination in favour of leadership by inspiration. This is why *talent* is next on the agility pyramid. If we lack purpose and the right culture, even the best talent will largely go to waste. Investing in talent acquisition and development in the face of a dysfunctional corporate culture is like planting a precious flower in contaminated soils. Some might survive or even grow a protective resilience, but most will wither away. Such organisations then proceed to scout for the next exotic growth to turn into collateral damage.

Talent needs healthy soil to flourish and grow. Great people enabled by a great culture can master any challenge. This is where we come to systems. Talking about structural transformation without the suitable ingredients in place will result in *agility theatre*, which is like *innovation theatre* but often more damaging. Whereas innovation theatre is more of a petting zoo where executives visit the innovation lab, sit in bean bags, and do fun things with sticky notes while admiring the casually-attired hipsteresque talent, *agility theatre* is typically staged to be more realistic and affects bigger portions of the organisation.

Structures follow from the most suitable environment serving the given purpose, reflecting the prevalent culture, and needed by its people to do the best work. Only when those structures have been worked out is it productive to talk about *technology* and how it might enable, and perhaps flexibly scale, all that goes well within the chosen structure, helping to support and evolve it in the most suitable form. Lastly, we get the dimension of *data*, allowing us to make the most of feedback loops, learn what's actually going on, and generate insights for meaningful enhancements; this facilitates the grounds for great performance and legitimises the purpose at the foundation of this pyramid.

> Structures follow from the most suitable environment serving the given purpose, reflecting the prevalent culture, and needed by its people to do the best work.

Non-agile organisations trying their luck at agile transformation like to turn this pyramid on its head – starting with data, technology, and structures. That means they will likely remain non-agile because no transformation starting from the above can be effective when a foundation of purpose, culture, and talent are lacking. I safely bet that if your organisation faces challenges *operationalising agile transformation*, its problems will boil down to the above (if not, I'll gladly invite you for a drink).

Just like people *once upon a time* created the corporate precedent and many of its managerial fairy tales that we are now challenging and looking to reinvent, *how we think* and *what we do* form the critical juncture in moving from today to what may be. Agile transformation is a bit of a misnomer. It actually describes *people transformation* facilitated by a surrounding context in which we can be our best. Imagine for a moment an F1 pit-stop scenario. The F1 car and driver arrive, and the race against the clock starts. Every second is extremely precious. If the said F1 pit stop team were practising non-agile ways of working, every mechanic changing a wheel or refilling the fuel would likely need to seek managerial approval before proceeding with their task; it would take forever. Agile philosophy and *jobs theory* teach us that focusing excessively on the process can mean we lose sight of the outcome, which is what ultimately counts. High-performing teams expanding the limit of what's humanly possible operate at a velocity in which they continuously face new opportunities and challenges that require them to act fast and in sync. Rigid procedures would simply get in the way. A highly peak-performing team defaults to trusting each member to perform because it's the only way for them to achieve the level they're playing at.

Beyond organisational agility, it's perhaps wise to re-embrace our human nature of being an agile species and translate that towards becoming an agile society and economy. It's our best shot at solving the pile-up of problems created by monolithic thinking and the socio-economic monoculture that inevitably follows. But the *RESET* we're looking for and

> It's perhaps wise to re-embrace our human nature of being an agile species and translate that towards becoming an agile society and economy.

describing here is going to take more than pressing a tiny little button as you might on your wi-fi router. But even small actions can materialise in a noticeable *delta* of positive and significant change. This is the spirit of encouragement to take away from these lines.

Invariably, it's our leadership and followership forming our future, shaping what's next, and driving our decisions forward. As we begin to ponder the interactions of fundamental human concepts covered here such as *purpose and pleasure, need and want, collaboration and self-interest, trust and scepticism*, we will discover new connections, insights, ideas, and ultimately solutions for our species and planet. While you may think and feel a certain way about these chapters, the story they seek to tell is perfectly evident once we focus our lens on the reality in front of us. It forces us to think of the ways in which we can preserve the good and graduate from the bad that defining human interaction and its many social and economic consequences. I am certain that a brighter, more liveable, and humane future will percolate from these reflections, and sincerely wish and hope that our global village will become more synchronised, peaceful, and happy as a result. There is a common path forward for humanity, offering us the opportunity to appreciate each other and resist the urge to meet each other with competition and hostility, cementing the foundation for an open, collaborative, and trusting status quo. This book is my contribution to the emerging movement that is manifesting a mental model in which social and economic fulfilment exist hand-in-hand. It's a light-touch instruction manual full of insights and ideas for how we can achieve it. Together, we'll *RESET* to a more aware present and promising future. I know you'll play your part in flying the flag of this new world order. Let's reap the ubiquitous benefits for you, me, and everyone around us....

V

a wonderful world

> The smallest privilege in the world being savoured is worth more than the greatest luxury remaining underappreciated.

EPILOGUE
How will all this shape our fates?

I t's tempting after this journeyed excursion through what is and what could be to side with Oscar Wilde and his priceless observation that *"we're all in the gutter, but some of us are looking at the stars"*.[1] Alternatively, we may find ourselves overwhelmed by the universe of possibilities between what's real today and what we could ideally be doing with all that we have at our disposal. This sense of awe at the monumental task ahead of us could make us inclined to herald Mark Twain's advice to *"not put off until tomorrow what can be put off till day-after-tomorrow just as well"*.[2] Truthfully, this book isn't going to mandate urgency like many voices have felt compelled to do. In line with the philosophy expressed throughout, I believe the greatest change emanates from motivation within. This means I've focused my energy on inspiring you to seek new horizons and inviting you to reflect on what is state of the art today. I'm certain the material in this book beautifully applies to the many strategies deployed at containing COVID-19 and their varied effectiveness in yielding desired results. As with all things, many different paths lead us to the destination, each coming with its own advantages and drawbacks. How the pandemic and narrative in this book will shape our fates, then, is truly in our hands. As a global professional speaker and keen observer of people, I've come to believe that we can truly tackle any challenge once we choose to *accept and want what the world needs from us.*

It's easy and tempting to bemoan what we are all going through at the moment. Some of us have been severely hit, some lightly affected, others had the fortune of discovering new opportunity amidst global chaos. My heartfelt empathy goes to all folks who live hand-to-mouth, who rely on national and global economic health as much as we collectively rely on human health. All of us must pledge to help those most affected through these times. But what about everyone of us who can still eat, buy stuff online and share memes and opinions across social media? How are we feeling about everything? Chances are there's a fair amount of resentment and frustration present within many right now, and I understand that. Freedom to live as you please is a fundamental right that feels tough to give up. But consider this: As many wise people have reiterated many times, true contentment and happiness are found independent of circumstance. It's about making peace with what is and keeping our inner world delightful no matter what. Few of us do this.

Personally (and especially as I am currently serving my return stay-home notice leading up to Christmas in Singapore) these past months have been a very welcome lesson in simplification. Those of you who know me better will be aware of my affinity towards minimalist and purist life philosophies. But when my travel routine was reduced from 20+ monthly travel days to zero, I understood what a simple life really amounted to: Making a lot fewer discretionary choices, and focusing on the quality of decisions over quantity of options. That is the beauty of constraints. As our offline lives are experiencing these new constraints, it is tempting to substitute some of our suspended freedom with overindulgence in the digital world. Inevitable and useful as it may be for work and socialising, the wise among us will seize the day in a newfound way. Suddenly, we are given freedom, space and perhaps time for checking in with ourselves and appreciating the most valuable aspects of our lives.

What I discovered almost immediately was that after initial agony, I started accepting life without my perpetual travel schedule. I realised freedom in sparing the daily commute and weekly packing, flying, transferring, checking in and out and so forth. I repurposed that time for cooking, yoga, meditating, thinking and writing. I continue evolving in this new reality and I am finding an unfamiliar joy return to the little things. It's as if this crisis amplified my senses and sensitised them to the nature and life happening all over. If we take a moment to appreciate how life in most of the world has rapidly adapted, we see unprecedented beauty and kindness in many places. Organisations are stepping up efforts around caring for customers, employees and stakeholders, governments are doing whatever they can and most of us are at least feeling a sense of shared plight. We are in this together.

What I really want to do today is to shape the conclusions you ultimately draw from all of it. How we remember these times, and what will happen once they pass is decided right now. Your reality going forward will be impacted by what we are experiencing today, and I believe there's so much we can learn about ourselves and life in this moment. What if there were a better, more resilient and happier you emerging from this all? I sincerely wish that you will find that reality for yourself, your social circles and your world. Call me an eternal optimist or an enlightened realist – I believe joy is in finding a way. In fact, it's time to make up for what was previously lacking.

Does it surprise us that we weren't perfectly prepared? Having downside protection in relation to an abstract scenario leaves a majority of people unbothered, simply because it's easier and more intuitive for many of us today to imagine tomorrow instead of an unlikely situation in an uncertain future. As the world got punched in the face by COVID-19, existing contingency plans didn't work brilliantly, probably because nobody thought it was purposeful or fun creating them in the first place. Generally speaking, we are bad at things we hardly care about. That also includes following rules we don't understand or perceive as useful. What resulted was a situation in which we needed to improvise, devising effective solutions fast. Gradually, governments and the private sector got up to speed. Now we have a plan and a common enemy, we still lack a consolidating purpose. We must realise enforcing new rules and compliance measures won't alone make people care about playing their part. Rules are rarely designed to be human centred, which is a problem if the intention is for people to follow them.

> Rules are rarely designed to be human centred, which is a problem if the intention is for people to follow them.

Following rules for fear of consequences is an extrinsic, highly reactive behaviour: We do it because we have to, often with a minimum effort approach. Beyond it what we really need is everyone to care about doing the right thing and that means moving beyond rules alone and focusing on the purpose in doing so. A rule is the equivalent of telling someone: actually, we don't trust you to do what is right, therefore we shall force you to do it. Rules are a necessary fallback when reason doesn't do the job, but they can't and shouldn't replace efforts to make people believe in behaving rightly. The way to reduce cigarette consumption isn't taxation or education alone, it's in swaying public opinion and social rituals around it such that they are less supportive of smoking behaviour. For that to happen, social dynamics need to compel people to consider such a shift worthwhile.

Bottom line: we must stop thinking rules will fix everything all by themselves. Mobilising as many as we can to champion the right behaviour should be an absolute priority. If we leave it at telling people what to do, it automatically makes them feel they're not in charge, which is dangerous especially in times like these. We need each and every contribution to solving the Coronavirus problem. Now we have urgency and rules to follow, let's address the glaringly obvious missing element that would connect humanity in this global fight: A powerful narrative uniting us. That will change everything and leave behind a better post-crisis world. It's a great opportunity for global society to grow back together on common terms. It's time to empower folks everywhere to feel they're part of the solution, not the problem. That means finding purpose in what we're going through today is going to make us more effective and happier in our efforts to recover from this global crisis as best as we can. It will hopefully leave us with a better humanity and might even inspire us to more decisive action in relation to climate change and other pressing global issues. I'd say it's well worth it.

The sacrifice we embrace or endure right now will mould us into an updated humanity. Repeat action is a great shortcut to habit formation. One thing is sure: life has changed beyond recognition. Whatever it will go back to eventually will create a new status quo. I'm positive it will be a good one. Just one example: digital transformation has been a 'priority' for years – only now are we seeing widespread efforts to make up for lost time. Organisations used to decision by committee are stepping up their game with surprising, perhaps uncomfortable, agility. But we must also see the bad. A sheer unbelievable portion of people are out of jobs, some without access to critical infrastructure or ability to meet their daily needs.

But beyond the pandemic, we are fighting an equally powerful global adversary: chronic disease. The rough figure globally for deaths due to such illnesses stands at 80%, almost irrespective of social and economic development. Most of humanity ultimately loses to chronic disease. It's just that epidemics like this one and less stellar healthcare systems accelerate the process considerably, and painfully.

What this means, with respect to the virus and beyond it, is that we all have the same core problem, but different timelines. Wealthier countries with better healthcare provision and correspondingly higher life expectancy simply delay the fatality of chronic conditions. But what if we went further than just improving our ways of coping with the impact of disease, and focused on preventing it altogether? Chronic diseases appear at all ages and for all types of reasons, but the main influencing factor is our lifestyle. We all know this, but healthy living has been a latent 'priority' in much the same way as digital transformation. It's wise to change that now. For instance, it is bizarre that in all the communication on the current situation, few speak about the importance of a healthy lifestyle in boosting immunity. That's like highlighting the devastating impact of cavities and the importance of brushing your teeth without giving much mention to the effects of sugar.

Our brains are engineered to prefer focusing on the short term and indulging quick fixes, but this is lopsided. Moderate diet and physical activity are a long-term intervention. Good hand hygiene and social distancing are also a form of prevention, but one that's squarely focused on the short term. No hand sanitising or quarantining in the world will reduce your risk of stroke, but ditching that junk food habit very well might. Compliance measures focused on keeping people apart should be the tip of the an iceberg of measures taken to recover public health in these trying times and ensure a better outcome the next time. That would require healthcare to transition from what we refer to as *'sick care'* to a focus on preventative action. This needs to happen at much greater scale. Much like a wave of fintechs emerged from the Global Financial Crisis, we should expect a drastic increase in digital health propositions focusing on preventative care and well-being to come our way.

Pulling it all together, there are many takeaways awaiting us still. It's time for a wholesome and considered approach to enter the way governments, organisations and people like you and me solve seemingly unsurmountable challenges. Our globalised world in the 2020s is far too complex to legitimate myopic problem-solving approaches. Issues like those presented by COVID-19 are deeply interconnected with the overall health of our system, exposing the need to understand the bigger picture and overall implications as an interconnected maze. Having courage to unbox big problems (and our thinking to address them) will give us a fighting chance at transforming our planet into a healthier home for humanity. However tempting it may be to jump at short-term fixes, stopping there would be dangerous. If we are to return to normal anytime soon and prevent similar scenarios in time to come, it's in our hands to be the change we ought to see, globally.

> Having courage to unbox big problems (and our thinking to address them) will give us a fighting chance at transforming our planet into a healthier home for humanity.

The current global outlook requires humanity to collaborate on a mega-scale to address one of the most significant challenges of modern times. As many of us know by now, such collaboration is only possible with a trusted (and trusting) foundation. Our best bet now is to break barriers and champion a shared global effort. We have a unique opportunity here to bring humanity together and neutralise the common enemy, in the hopes that the effects will outlast the crisis and set a new precedent for global economic and social harmony.

That's my Christmas wish for 2020. As you read this in 2021, I hope it has begun to ring true.

Warmest regards,
Philipp Kristian Diekhöner
Sunday, 20 December 2020

Endnotes

1   Oscar Wilde, *Lady Windermere's Fan.*
2   *More Maxims of Mark,* Johnson, 1927.

ACKNOWLEDGEMENTS

You give from what you have, not from what you lack.

M any everyday heroines and heroes have added their magic touches to this book. I am extremely grateful for their contributions. My heartfelt thanks to all of you. My efforts are greatly amplified by this wonderful community of people.

There's Lindsey Palma Malcolm, who passionately and painstakingly edited a first rough version of this manuscript. Her comprehensive suggestions and commentary felt like a quantum leap. They are the work of a savant driven by deep appreciation of the art and science of storytelling.

Next, Kenny Gan, who made the initial introduction to WSP. As one of my longest standing booking agents, he has significantly influenced the impact of my work, by evangelising it with his eminent clientele and network in Asia.

I also thank Yee-Hong Khoo, Sandhya Venkatesh, Yulin Jiang, Jimmy Low, Triena Ong and everyone else at WSP for their dedicated and highly professional work on this book project (mentioned in order of my interaction with them).

Further thanks goes to Michael Low and Sarah Yip from SMU Academy for giving me opportunity to share my knowledge. This sparked the idea for a book reflecting the essence of my work.

A very special thanks also goes to all of my cherished clientele who have continued to support me with their business, in a year defined by crisis and uncertainty.

Equally, my thanks goes to my parents for encouragement. It was insightful to spend more time together in 2020 than in prior years of perpetual travelling.

I'm thankful as well to have been introduced to the artistic talents of Eva Azpurua, who designed and illustrated the book cover together with the team at WSP and myself.

I just as much recognise everyone else who provided input and counsel in relation to this book and who lent moral support and inspiration. You know who you are!

I also extend my deep gratitude to Singapore for being my wonderful home in Asia in the past decade. I owe so much to this country, its people and

I also extend my deep gratitude to Singapore for being my wonderful home in Asia in the past decade. I owe so much to this country, its people and government. More than ever, I am happy to have found a base, place and purpose here.

government. More than ever, I am happy to have found a base, place and purpose here.

Finally, and most important of all, my infinite appreciation for the work of God on earth and in my own life is the guiding light and red thread in my world. I am most grateful for this daily inspiration and reminder to live my best life, in service of the greater good. I hope my life's work resonates, illuminates and impacts yours, and I look forward to keep learning.

Thank you, everyone, for making such a positive difference. Thank you for making all of this possible.

INDEX